Laity

in the

Church

and in the

World

RESOURCES FOR
ECUMENICAL DIALOGUE

THE ROMAN CATHOLIC—PRESBYTERIAN/REFORMED CONSULTATION

At its April 1995 meeting, the Roman Catholic/Presbyterian–Reformed Consultation reviewed and approved the publication of this jointly prepared volume. In our ongoing consultation this was the fifth round of meetings, each devoted to specifically chosen topics. This round was co-chaired by Bishop John S. Cummins of the Bishops' Committee for Ecumenical and Interreligious Affairs and by Dr. Catherine Gunsalus Gonzalez of the Presbyterian Church (USA), who have jointly written the introduction to the book as well as making substantial contributions to its contents. It has been reviewed by Bishop Alexander J. Brunett, Chairman of the Bishops' Committee for Ecumenical and Interreligious Affairs and is authorized for publication by the under-signed.

Monsignor Dennis M. Schnurr
General Secretary
NCCB/USCC

First Printing, May 1998

ISBN 1-57455-247-3

CONTENTS

INTRODUCTION

We are pleased to present to our congregations in both the Roman Catholic and the Presbyterian/Reformed communities this instrument for ecumenical dialogue on the *Laity in the Church and in the World*. The papers that follow are the joint effort of the representatives to the Roman Catholic—Presbyterian/Reformed Consultation and flow from its Round V (1992–1995) series of dialogues.

Begun in 1965, these pioneering discussions (rounds) have spoken to such central ecumenical topics as "Revelation, Scripture, and Tradition"; "Ministry and Order in the Church"; "Women in the Church"; and "Whether Social and Ethical Issues Are Today as Church Dividing as Doctrinal Issues Were in the Sixteenth Century." This last involved careful dealing with such sensitive topics as peace and nuclear deterrence, human rights in South Africa and America, abortion, and aid to private education. (A more complete history of the consultation over the years is given in Part Two of this book.)

In Round V, our group decided against writing a treatise. We felt that discussion had been profitable for us through the three years of conversations. After so many years of separation, we realized the realities of unfamiliarity, apprehension, and incomplete or inaccurate assumptions. We have gained much from the instruction and clarification, and we wish to share with you the reader what one of our members has called "the excitement of mutual discovery."

We chose to prepare something for our church leadership. The presentations, therefore, are not geared toward effortless reading. However, we feel they will correspond to the talents and interest of those who take their faith—and the intellectual side of it—with great seriousness.

The subjects are the underlying common theologies; the issue of authority as an aid to Christian life; a particularly insightful appraisal of contemporary relations in society that have powerful ecumenical implications; some tools to help in the dialogue; and an analysis of religious words common to us by frequency of usage but not identical in meaning conveyed.

Our thanks to the sponsoring organizations: the Caribbean and North American Council of the World Alliance of Reformed Churches (CANAAC) and the National Conference of Catholic Bishops (NCCB). We are grateful to the staff people representing those organizations, Rev. Margarethe B. J. Brown for CANAAC and Dr. Eugene J. Fisher for the NCCB.

We offer this book in gratitude for our own opportunities together and in the hope that it will aid toward the unity we seek and to which, we, in our day, are being called by the Spirit.

Most Rev. John S. Cummins
Bishop of Oakland

Dr. Catherine Gunsalus Gonzalez
Columbia Theological Seminary

Co-chairs for Round V

ACKNOWLEDGMENTS

Dr. Catherine Gunsalus Gonzalez (Columbia Theological Seminary in Atlanta, Ga.) and Bishop John S. Cummins (Oakland, Calif.) co-chaired the teams for Round V, which consisted of the following members:

For the CANAAC, Dr. David Beeson (United Church of Christ, Jefferson, Md.); Rev. Paul Janssen (Reformed Church in America, Park Ridge, N.J.); Dr. Alice Ling (Bangor Theological Seminary, Hanover, N.II.); Ms. Allie Latimer, Esq. (Presbyterian Church, USA, Washington, D.C.); and Mr. Harold Saunders (Director of International Affairs, Kettering Foundation, Washington, D.C.).

For the NCCB: Dr. Eugene J. Fisher (NCCB Staff); Dr. John Collins Harvey (Georgetown University Center for Clinical Ethics, Washington, D.C.); Bro. Jeffrey Gros, FSC (Secretariat for Ecumenical and Interreligious Affairs, Washington, D.C.); Dr. Dolores Leckey (former director of the Secretariat for the Laity, Washington, D.C.); and Rev. Kenan Osborne, OFM (Franciscan School of Theology, Berkely, Calif.).

Part One

THEOLOGY, ECUMENISM, AND THE ROLE OF THE LAY CHRISTIAN

Chapter One

EPIGRAPH

The sessions between the Presbyterian/Reformed Churches and the Roman Catholic Church on the lay person were very exciting. However, from the start, both sides realized that one cannot immediately discuss the role of the lay person in the Church. As a result, we decided on an initial section that dealt with important background issues: namely, who is Jesus (christology) and what is the Church (ecclesiology). We realized that there are many contemporary ways of looking at Jesus and many ways of looking at the Church. The following few pages simply outline some of the most important ways of considering Jesus today and of considering a Church that is in the process of seeking unity. We urge that you read these pages carefully, and if you are having a discussion, that your discussion of the lay person in the Church begin with a round-table sharing of what each of you believes about Jesus and believes about the Church. Only then should you move on to the main theme: the lay person in the Church today.

For Reflection:

With strong traditions of authority both in Presbyterian/Reformed Churches and the Roman Catholic Church, is there hope of great harmony between the two understandings?

Would it be valuable to trace further the impact of Western European history and culture on congregational life in the Presbyterian/Reformed Churches and in the Roman Catholic Church?

In the American context, does there need to be a refreshing of the Pauline understanding of authority as a gift to the Church?

Chapter One

THE ROLE OF THE LAY CHRISTIAN

by Kenan B. Osborne, OFM

Preliminary Considerations

An ecumenical discussion on the role of the lay Christian involves many preliminary or background considerations. Most of these considerations provide the underlying basis for the conclusions that such an ecumenical discussion might develop. These underlying considerations operate as presuppositions and, therefore, do not generally become the central focus of the discussion.

This present committee has selected two major issues that provide such preliminary or background status: Jesus (christology) and the Church (ecclesiology).

Every theological study of the lay Christian is based on the meaning of Church. The meaning of Church, however, rests on the meaning of Jesus.

Christology

Jesus is central to Christian faith:

> Hence, it was necessary for the Son of God to become for us "Immanuel, that is, God with us" (Is 7:14; Mt 1:23), and in such a way that his divinity and our human nature might by mutual connection grow together. Otherwise, the nearness would not have been near enough nor the affinity sufficiently firm, for us to hope that God might dwell with us (Calvin, *Institutes II*, xii, 1).

> Christ is the light of humanity. . . . All men and women are called to this union with Christ, who is the light of the world, from whom we go forth, through whom we live, and towards

whom our whole life is directed (*Lumen Gentium*, Vatican II Documents, 1, 1 and 3).

The centrality of Jesus for our Christian faith and our Christian life is at the heart of our ecumenical dialogues. However, a mere mention that Jesus and the study of Jesus (christology) are basic to our common faith is itself open to further dialogue. This present committee realizes quite keenly that in the theological world of our present day, major christological studies have taken place so that one must continuously ask: Which Jesus is at the center of our Christian faith and life?

Although an exhaustive listing of these various contemporary christological discussions is not apposite to our specific theme on the lay Christian, the committee is well aware that in today's theological world, several important emphases in christological writings have been developed over the past century. Each different emphasis in christology tends to influence—at least in an indirect way—various emphases that pervade a study of the Church—an ecclesiology. The influence of these various christologies on ecclesiology is subtle, tending to highlight a social dimension, a feminist dimension, an ecumenical dimension, and so forth. The following list indicates the main emphases that have been presented by various groups of scholars—Protestant and Catholic.

The resurrection of Jesus has been, perhaps, the one issue that has received the lion's share of theological investigation (Fuller, Dufour). The studies on the resurrection of Jesus have theologically altered, in many ways, the traditional presentations of the life and death of Jesus. In European christology during the middle of the twentieth century, the resurrection was frequently considered the point of departure for christology (Rahner, Pannenberg). Both in theology and spirituality, the transition from cross to resurrection became a major part of the discussion.

The liberation theology of South America (Gutiérrez, Boff, Sobrino, Bonino) has raised two major issues for current christology: the social dimension of the Gospel, on the one hand, and the acculturation of theology, on the other. In both Protestant and Roman Catholic theology, these two issues of liberation theology have had a profound impact on ecclesiology.

Feminist theology, which by and large has not directly focused on Jesus but rather on the issues of God and the Church, has indirectly, but still quite strongly, challenged the way in which christology and ecclesiology have been presented by both the Reformed and Roman Catholic Churches (Ruether, Schlusser-Fiorenza). The many ramifications of feminist theology on christology and ecclesiology have still to be worked out.

Jesus and Judaism has, more recently, become a major theme within christology (Charlesworth, Sanders, Meier, Crossan). This study, with its sociological and historical analyses, has recast much of the traditional presentations on Jesus, especially in areas of historical detail.

New Testament hermeneutics have clearly altered the way in which one pursues christology. From Bultmann to the post-Bultmannians, the scholarly reading of the New Testament has wrestled continuously with the historical issues and the faith issues involved in these writings (Bultmann, Bornkamm, Jeremias, Perrin, Borg, Schillebeeckx). Although the material on the Jesus of history and the Christ of faith has moved considerably since the time of Kähler, the issue itself remains operative in christology today.

The globalization of theology has also had a major effect on christology, (Hick, Schreiter). Although the portrait of a Jewish Jesus is itself a very inculturated event, Jesus, today, is presented by both the Reformed and Roman Catholic Churches as a universal event, of crucial importance for all cultures.

It is remarkable that the theologians who have developed these several christologies are ecumenical, that is, the theologians are both Protestant and Roman Catholic, and they have worked in dialogue with each other, rather than simply using each other's works.

Even though these and other currents within the christological studies today make a "common" christology almost impossible to attain—even within a given denomination, much less within an ecumenical dialogue—this present committee, which has been charged to consider the lay Christian in today's Church and world, reaffirms that Jesus is central to Christian faith and life and therefore is central to any discussion on the role of the lay Christian in the Church and in the world. The precise way in which Jesus is central may move either along confessional lines or along various theological lines. Still, it is clear that the current richness of various christological thinking has challenged all of the Churches.

The centrality of Jesus for Christian life does allow us to formulate, at least in a general way, the following basic christological positions, which will govern our study of the lay Christian in the Church and in the world.

The central message of Jesus' preaching was the kingdom or reign of God. The teaching on the reign of God, therefore, cannot help but be at the very heart of the Church, particularly in the Church's preaching and in the Church's administration of the sacraments. This mystery of God's reign at the very heart of the Church allows the Church to be an instrument of spiritual transformation, not only of the Church itself but also of society. The Church, in all its manifestations of God's reign, becomes a profound source of new life and new spiritual potential within the human community.

The biblical message of Jesus, in which one finds the very revelation of God's word, governs the existence of the Church; the Church is a servant of the word of God. This word of God must be interpreted again and again by each and every generation of the Christian community, for it is a living word and a life-giving word. The lay Christian, in a very special way, becomes the bearer of this word both to fellow Christians and to fellow humans.

Not only does a worshiping community of the Church offer, through grace, an understanding of the revealed word of God for our times, but the leadership members of a church community, as well as the scholarly members of a church community, participate strongly in the life of the Spirit, as the Gospel of John indicates: "When, however, the Spirit comes, who reveals the truth about God, he will lead you into all the truth. He will not speak on his own authority, but he will speak of what he hears and will tell you of things to come" (Jn 16:13).

Although the reign of God is the central message of the teaching of Jesus, Jesus continuously taught that this very reign was present beyond the accepted limits of his time. In widening the scope of God's reign to those who were socially and religiously rejected, Jesus was clearly presenting an understanding of God, who was forgiving in ways that went to those in the by-ways and the hedgerows of life, to the marginated, and the little ones of this earth. Moreover, Jesus was a healer, bringing physical and spiritual health to those who were often considered unclean. In many ways, this barrier-breaking aspect of Jesus' preaching and healing has remained one of the most challenging issues of the Christian message. Each new generation of Christians has had to struggle to face the bias, the prejudice, and the discrimination, both within the Church itself and throughout the larger world. The good news—the Gospel—preached to the poor and the marginated, transforms the message of Jesus into a powerful social message for every age.

In all of this, the mystery of the Church has again and again been an agent of renewal and transformation in society. The resurgent power of the Church has been the power of God's holy grace and the presence of the Holy Spirit, so that time and time again, the Church, in its best moments, has clearly been the yeast in the dough, the city on the hill, the light of all nations. Lay Christians share deeply in this mystery of Jesus, which is also the mystery of the Church. They become the yeast, the city, and the light.

Ecclesiology

At the time of the Reformation a systematic theology of the Church— what we today call an ecclesiology—was just beginning to appear in the academic world. John Calvin was a strong force for this development, and the Council of Trent also nourished the formulation of such a systematic presentation of the Church. However, it was in the two succeeding centuries after the Reformation and the Council of Trent, that the systematic study of the Church—ecclesiology—began to develop in a very comprehensive way.

The various theologies of the Church, which subsequently were developed, moved along differing lines, often reflecting specific key issues that had either been central at the beginning of the Reformation or had become central as the individual Churches polarized, once the division of the Church had taken place.

Some of the major theologies of the Church developed on the basis of the following themes:

A covenantal understanding of the Church, which found its basis in a covenant theology *per se*. This emphasis on the covenant goes back to early Jewish roots, but was also developed by the *de potentia Dei absoluta* (the absolute power of God) theology of the fifteenth century, just prior to the Reformation. In this ecclesiology, the stress falls on God's election through grace and a subsequent covenanted response between God and the community. In such a theology, the role of the lay person is key, based on baptism, the very sign of the covenant. Based on God's loving grace, the entirety of the Church is covenantal: the Word of God in scripture speaks of this covenant; the structures of the Church are born from covenantal grace; the promise of God is sealed in the promise of the covenant.

A christologically historical understanding of the Church, which, in one of its several forms, stressed the role of Jesus, gathering his disciples, selecting the Twelve, and empowering Peter and the Twelve to be the "rulers of the Church." In this ecclesiology, the hierarchical structure of the Church has, at times, been overdrawn, so that the lay Christian has only a secondary or derivative role within the Christian community. Contemporary exegetical studies have indeed modified this approach to ecclesiology, as one finds, for instance, in the systematic structure of *Lumen Gentium* (*Constitution on the Church in the Modern World*), the document developed at the second Vatican Council. In this document, the mystery of the Church is first expressed, followed by the mystery of every Christian life, the People of God. Only then is there a discussion of hierarchy and specific lay ministries.

An understanding of the Church centered in the Holy Spirit, or a view of the Church that gives central emphasis to the role of the Holy Spirit. In this approach, the Pentecost event in the lives of the first disciples of Jesus finds an echo in every succeeding generation of Christians. Each Christian community, sharing in this Pentecost grace, receives anew the empowering Spirit of God, so that each Christian becomes an evangelizer of the good news, a witness to the word of God. Indeed, this is not a new understanding of the Church, but one that goes back to the earliest of church times, for the centralizing presence of the Holy Spirit pervades the theology of Church that one finds among all the Eastern Churches. One finds this same centralizing emphasis on the Holy Spirit in the charismatic and pentecostal Churches of the West, and in the Reformed tradition, the Holy Spirit is key to the very meaning of Church.

A trinitarian understanding of the Church, which in contemporary discussion opens the Christian community to the operation of the trinitarian God within the entire world, including other religions. In this ecclesiology, the focus centers on the trinitarian God at the center of all creation, and thereby the issue of interreligious dialogue becomes acute. In this approach, new depths of meaning are found in the very concepts of reign and of Church. In developing this form of ecclesiology, the term *koinonia* (community) has taken on a profound significance, for what we all share in common through the grace of God is now seen as a major treasure of our human life, and this *koinonia*—this common treasure that we all share from one and the same triune God—calls for transformation, both of the individual and of society. Lay Christians are witnesses of a theo-ecological world. Each baptized person individually, and the Church as a community, is called on to discern the work of the Spirit throughout the entire earth. They are all witnesses of God's *koinonia* and thus together form a community called Church, an ecclesial *koinonia*.

Since there are several theological ways of looking at the Church, all of which have validity, the present committee has not opted to base its position on the lay Christian either exclusively or predominantly on any one of these various approaches to a theology of Church. However, certain issues have been selected by the committee as guidelines for its discussion on the lay person in the Church. These issues are the following:

All men and women in the Church have a baptismal equality. Neither gender nor race nor culture makes certain Christians superior or inferior. Discipleship is a common matrix for all baptized, for all are the People of God, the covenanted people, and baptism is the sign of this holy covenant.

Ordained ministry or priesthood is itself a special grace and gift of God, but it is intimately related to the priesthood of all believers. The ordained ministers of the Church, in both the Reformed and Roman Catholic traditions, are called by God to be servant leaders of the Church.

The distinction of lay/cleric has gradually become a part of Christian tradition. Although the terms, as we know them today, are not part of the New Testament, they have become special terms that help us understand the one Lord who calls in different ways.

Although a rite of ordination emerges gradually in the early Church, both the Reformed Church and the Roman Catholic Church hold the rite of ordination in a special way. In both Churches, however, there is a stress on an inner call and an outer call. In both, there is a holiness—a working of the Spirit of God—in the calling to ministry.

Every Christian, whether ordained or lay, lives out his or her life within several dimensions: a social dimension as he or she participates in the secular world; an institutional dimension as he or she shares in the work of the structured Church; a theological dimension as he or she meditates on the meaning of the Christ event; a spiritual dimension as he or she is transformed by the Holy Spirit.

The above discussion on christology and ecclesiology represents background material for this committee's presentation of the lay person in the Church. Such background must be considered simply as working presuppositions. They will, however, shape the way this document is structured and formulated.

Chapter Two

EPIGRAPH

The two chairs of these sessions, Bishop John S. Cummins for the Roman Catholic position, and Professor Catherine Gunsalus Gonzalez, faced a most important issue: the question of authority within a Reformed tradition and within a Roman Catholic tradition. Lay people, in each tradition, play a quite different role. Unless this is understood carefully, no dialogue is possible. There are indeed common roots from the New Testament, but there have been traditions of long standing that nuance how each Christian community views the role of the lay person, authority, and the clerical person. Once more this is serious background for a dialogue on the lay person in today's ecumenical church efforts, and the committee invites you to read this section with great care and with great openness.

Chapter Two

CHURCH AUTHORITY
AND THE LAITY

by Bishop John S. Cummins (Catholic Perspective)
Dr. Catherine Gunsalus Gonzalez (Reformed Perspective)

Common Roots, Common Concepts

The Catholic, Presbyterian, and Reformed Churches today all have visible governing structures, though these show many variations in both form and degree of authority. Catholics, for example, have a hierarchical system based on bishops, while governance in the United Church of Christ is based on the local congregation. Yet all the groups participating in this dialogue share many common notions about what church authority is and what it is supposed to do.

At his Ascension, the Lord Jesus proclaimed to his disciples, "All authority in heaven and on earth has been given to me. Go therefore and make disciples of all nations, baptizing them in the name of the Father and of the Son and of the Holy Spirit, and teaching them to obey everything that I have commanded you" (Mt 28:18–20, NRSV, as are all scriptural quotations in this chapter). So from the very beginning, the Lord associated his own universal authority with the mission of the Church. And Christians view human governing structures in the Church as justified by the Lord's mandate.

We need, however, to say why there can be distinctions of power within the Church, because at the most fundamental level, all believers are equal. St. Paul says, "Now that faith has come, we are no longer subject to a disciplinarian, for in Christ Jesus you are all children of God through faith. As many of you as were baptized into Christ have clothed your-selves with Christ. There is no longer Jew or Greek, there is no longer slave or free, there is no longer male or female; for all of you are one in Christ Jesus" (Gal 3:25–28).

Yet in St. Paul's letters and elsewhere, we do not find an early Christian community existing without any internal structure or differentiation of roles. Instead, we find authority presented as a gift to the Church and a reality in service to it. At the same time, the exact form this authority takes in the New Testament era is far from clear. We read of apostles, prophets, deacons, and presbyters (elders), for example, but both the scope of their roles and how those roles related to each other are not easy to spell out.

So far, we have seen that churches view their organizational forms as helping them to carry out the mission entrusted to them. It is important to realize that this mission has one primary objective: to bring human beings—every single one—into a personal relationship with the Lord Jesus Christ, and through Jesus, into unfailing communion with God. We can detect two principal means by which the Church carries out this mission. First is the proclamation of the word of God that has come to us in the form of the Bible. Through the reading, studying, and praying of these ancient texts, the Holy Spirit here and now, wherever that might be, brings Jesus into our presence.

The second means is the Church itself, an assembly of believers, a com-munity of faith that is the Body of Christ in the world at this moment. St. Paul wrote "For just as the body is one and has many members, and all the members of the body, though many, are one body, so it is with Christ. For in the one Spirit we were all baptized into one body. Now you are the body of Christ and individually members of it" (1 Cor 12:12–13, 27). For Christians, this is more than poetic language. It means that the Church is not only a sign of the presence of Jesus in our world today, it actually is what it symbolizes, the presence of the Risen Lord in all his power to heal and give life. (Catholics call such a sign a *sacrament.*)

Because the Church, though of divine origin, is a human society, it has the traits of any human social organization or group. Among these are structures of authority, including roles that involve decisions about policies, plus the basic powers to make and enforce rules for the common good of the group and the more effective achievement of its goals. It is really no surprise, then, to find such roles present in the Christian Church from the outset.

The Lord Jesus, however, commands Christians to exercise authority in the Church in a way different from that seen in other human groups, where too often ". . . their great ones are tyrants over them. It will not be so among you; but whoever wishes to be great among you must be your servant, and whoever wishes to be first among you must be your slave" (Mt 20:20–25). So when a differentiation of roles entered that original equality of believers as one in the Lord, it involved not the elevation of human leaders over the faithful, but the charging of structured leadership with a ministry of service to help all Christians carry out the joyful task of bringing the Lord to one another and to the world.

A Catholic Perspective

Catholic Powers That Be

The clearest office having authority visible in the early Church is that of *apostle*. The Twelve chosen by Jesus ministered to the community by witnessing to the resurrection at worship, but they also had power in daily life to set down rules, to provide leadership, and to exercise judicial powers. Already in Acts their number is restored when the Eleven choose Mathias by lot (Acts 1:15–26). This suggests an institution, that is, a permanent structure intended by the Lord to exist over time even though individual members of it will be replaced. The fact that St. Paul and others who did not meet Jesus during his lifetime could later nonetheless come to be called apostles too, shows that the role of apostle was never limited only to those very first disciples named by Jesus in the Gospels.

Catholics believe that the Lord Jesus intended the institution of the Twelve Apostles to continue as long as the Church exists in this world as a shared ministry of authority. We further believe that the early church officials known as *episcopoi* (overseers) in Greek, and now called *bishops,* as a group constitute at any given time in history the institution in which the ministry of the Twelve continues. This is what we mean by *apostolic* succession. At one time, it was thought necessary in Catholic theology to trace each bishop back in a direct line to one of the Twelve, if such a thing were possible. But now many conclude that this would not be required if we think of the body of bishops as a group ministry handed down from one generation to the next.

The ministry of the group—or *college*—of bishops, continues the apostolic role of service to the entire assembly of the faithful. Its purpose is to empower and enable all members of the Church to lead their lives, according to their own special charisms and ministries, each one contributing her or his part in the overall constant mission of mediating God's love to human beings through the Lord Jesus.

Catholics also believe that Jesus gave St. Peter a special role of authority among the Twelve. There is evidence of this, for example, in Matthew 16:18, "You are Rock (*Petros,* in Greek) and on this rock (*petra*) I will build my Church." According to very ancient traditions, now given support by archaeological evidence, St. Peter ministered finally at Rome and was martyred there. This gave rise to the understanding that the bishop who succeeds to this Roman ministry also succeeds to that special authority conferred by the Lord on St. Peter. The traditional title for this office, based on the Latin word *papa* (father), is pope.

Here it will be helpful to make some distinctions. The first will be more familiar to those in the Presbyterian and Reformed traditions. It is the distinction between authority and governance in the Church. *Authority* in a religious framework concerns claims made on our faith. It determines what is part of Christian faith, and what is not. The source of such authority is the Holy Spirit. *Governance,* on the other hand, means the actual concrete form of organizing a church's day-to-day life.

In the Catholic Church the basic powers to exercise both authority and governance belong to the group or college of bishops in union with the pope, and we are accustomed to use the word *authority* to include both functions. When Catholics want to emphasize authority as the power to decide what is true teaching and what is not, we use the term *magisterium.* Strictly speaking, the Holy Spirit guides the entire community of the faithful in true belief. But for Catholics, only the college of bishops in union with the pope may bring to the surface specific teachings, or rather, declare that such teachings are the universal belief of the Church.

The pope and bishops together are also in charge of governance in the Catholic Church. Ultimately, the buck stops with them when it comes to the making of regulations for the common good, the carrying out of those regulations, and decisions about the breaking of those regulations. But unlike the magisterium, which may not be delegated to others, the pope and bishops can and do delegate their power of governance. In fact, the size of the Catholic Church would make it impossible for them not to do so.

Now we need to make another distinction, that between clergy and laity. All bishops are members of the clergy, but they are not the only ones in that group. The distinction between clergy and laity arises from the activity in which the Church finds its fullest expression, the liturgy, that is, the community assembled for worship.

Within the worshiping assembly there are various roles or ministries. One of these is to provide for an orderly celebration, and this is the task of the presiders. When the community of believers disperses after worship, the ministerial roles continue, including that of providing *order*, only now it is order in everyday Christian life. Catholics believe the Lord Jesus provided the Church with a sacrament of governance, and the sacrament is logically known, then, as *holy orders*. People who receive the sacrament of holy orders are clergy; people who do not are laity.

Besides the order of bishop, there are two others: priest and deacon. The role of the *priest* was only gradually distinguished from that of the bishop. Early Christian communities soon grew too large for the bishop alone to lead in worship. People called *elders* became the bishop's "stand-ins." The Greek word for elder is *presbyter,* from which the Presbyterian Church derives its name. Members of all churches participating in this dialogue may be surprised to learn that *priest* is simply another form of the same word.

Deacons in the early Church were also associated with bishops, but not in the realm of worship. Originally they concerned themselves with practical details of the community's life. Acts 6:1–6 tells how the apostles chose the first seven deacons to make sure that everybody in the Jerusalem church had enough to eat. Deacons, over time, became the bishop's primary agents in matters of secular life involving the Church. In fact, for several hundred years they exercised a degree of authority in such temporal matters often far exceeding that of priests and even bishops. But then cultural developments seem to have been the main factor in an evolution that led to the virtual disappearance of deacon ministry in the Catholic Church. Until recently, it had become merely the last stepping stone on the path to priestly ordination, even if still considered along with the offices of bishop and priest as part of the sacrament of holy orders.

Priests and deacons, because of their close connection with the bishops both historically and sacramentally, have a sort of natural share in church governance. But they are not now and never have been the only ones to share such responsibilities. Members of the Catholic laity have always participated in administration and other activities necessary for the life and mission of the Church.

We have noted that the Church becomes most perfectly visible in the liturgy. The Church does not exist for the liturgy, however, but the liturgy for the Church and her mission. That mission means proclaiming the Gospel outside the Christian *community* assembled for worship. While this may take the form of overt preaching, the greatest activity concerned here is the witness of Christian lives. And most of these lives are those of lay people. So while clergy have a specific role of continuing to focus the *community's* visible presence for the world outside of liturgy, the actual presence and mission are accomplished by the laity as they are spread like leaven throughout the world's daily life.

If clergy serve the community in worship, they also serve the community as it carries out its mission to the world. But here their role is less like that of political authorities and more like that of coaches—to provide a kind of leadership that enables lay people to first recognize their calling to preach the Gospel by their lives and second to develop the spiritual skills and cooperative team spirit essential to that task. Whenever church leaders, whether clergy or laity, narrow the vision of their role in favor of some authoritarian functionalism, they distort and harm the mission of the Church. Catholic theology clearly acknowledges the broader notion of helping the laity fulfill their mission when it speaks of clerical roles as ones of service to the community, and Catholic custom does so at the highest level when it refers to the pope as *servus servorum Dei,* that is, "servant of the servants of God."

Bumps on the Road to Unity

For Americans who are not Catholics, the structure of authority in the Catholic Church can seem at once quite simple and quite unappealing. Though we have moved so far beyond the hostility that still characterized the recent past, to many the Catholic Church must seem simple because it is run by a male hierarchy with supreme authority vested in one individual, the pope. No doubt it seems unappealing for the same reason. How in this age of democracy can such an organization claim to represent the Lord Jesus, who brought us freedom? It must be even more confusing to notice that the lingering views of Catholic authority do not quite match the reality evident since the Second Vatican Council.

It is here that a brief look at history can be of great help for non-Catholics and Catholics alike. To understand where the road to unity is leading us, we need to know where we have been. We think we know, but we are often mistaken. For example, to criticize Catholics for being hostile to democratic procedures ignores the fact that neither Luther nor Calvin had any concept like the individualism of twentieth century America. Calvin certainly did not intend to form a denomination. He wished to reform the Roman Catholic Church, the only Church he knew. Yet he ended up in Geneva with an authoritarian system so severe that no one today would accept it.

Aside from the exclusion of women from ordained ministry, which we will not attempt to deal with here, the two areas that probably present non-Catholics with the biggest problems in Catholic authority structures are the hierarchy of bishops and the vast power of the pope. Both, but especially the papacy, are regarded by many Protestants as monolithic entities unchanged for 2,000 years and functioning in a dictatorial fashion that has kept the laity in a state of blind obedience, if not outright subservience. A brief look at history belies these notions.

Over the ages, the basic unit of the Catholic Church has remained the local church united around the bishop. But the actual manner of structuring local churches has hardly been uniform. Many and various approaches have been used. Very often leadership has chosen a conciliar approach, meaning a system that involves consultation and collaboration. This conciliarity at the local level reflects the manner in which the ancient regional churches, through their bishops, cooperated with each other on a wider scale.

From the earliest times, it was the practice of bishops in various regions to meet at local church councils, or *synods,* to deal with issues of common concern to their particular areas. Such synods did not meet regularly, but only as the need arose. Both matters of theology and discipline were the subjects of discussion and common action. While each bishop exercised autonomy in his own region, the decisions of councils could call local bishops to account. A regional council could have an impact on the whole Church if recognized as a general council. Very early also the approval of the pope, if not his direct involvement, was a key factor in the acceptance of conciliar actions.

Especially after the time of Constantine, and while the Roman Empire endured in the Western Mediterranean, synods were by no means secret meetings of bishops without reference to their communities. Lay involvement was and always has been part of church councils, although less so since the high Middle Ages. Exerting great influence, too, were the monks and nuns, abbesses and abbots of religious communities. Although even many Catholics are accustomed to think of these people as part of the clergy, technically they have always been considered laity, unless ordained as priests or deacons.

We know more clearly today than ever before the extent to which specific features of its cultural environment in Western Europe have affected the Church's life. Many suggest, for example, that a rigid differentiation between clergy and laity grew in response to the efforts of the Roman Empire on several occasions to oppress and even exterminate the Christian community. A strict military type regimen, reflecting the organizing principle of the empire itself, was perhaps necessary for survival and growth in a hostile world. Once Constantine established Christianity as the religion of the empire, the Church spontaneously adopted Roman political forms. To this day, a bishop heads a *diocese,* even as the Romans divided their territory into administrative units of the same name.

When the empire collapsed under the weight of its own decay and the invasions from the north, bishops were often required by default to assume political responsibilities. Thus began an even closer collaboration of Church and state that was necessary at the moment, but not without adverse consequences later. It was also in this period that the political power of the pope began to grow dramatically. As bishop of the surviving Roman culture's Mother City, the pope was a microcosm of what Western Europe was depending on the whole Church for—social stability and safety.

Post-Roman Europe was a place of anarchy and violence. Political power went to the strongest. What had been a vast area of unified trade and culture fragmented into hundreds of small territories controlled by local bosses. The Church was the only institution capable of providing enough unity to start society on the long road back to civil order. In assuming this task, the Church also began to get severely entangled in secular politics. But it is important to avoid simplistic understandings of what happened.

A case in point would be the issue of "clericalization." Often seen in second-guessing hindsight as a diminishing of lay power within the Church, it was more likely the exact opposite—an attempt to gain the liberty of both clergy *and* laity from the feudal or imperial secular powers of the day. The laity were excluded from some decision making, for example, after the Gregorian reform of the 1050s, so that the Church and not the civil rulers could invest bishops with their authority for service of the Gospel rather than for service of the state. Similarly, papal authority developed to support the freedom of the Western churches over and against the feudal princes.

For long periods of time in Europe one of the safest and most productive forms of life was monastic. Religious communities living apart from society were often the last and only bulwark against violence and injustice. The brilliant and dedicated work of monastic copyists helped preserve not only the Scriptures, but much classical learning. Still, the monastic approach to life emphasizes the coming of the Kingdom of God in its fullness at the end of the world. When the chaos of society makes it seem like the end has arrived, monasticism is a proper emphasis. At other times, it may distract from aspects of the Church's mission. This may explain why religious orders like the Franciscans, whose members live in a community but who do not withdraw from the world, came into being. With one foot in the monastic tradition but the other firmly planted in social action, such groups may have arisen in response to an undue influence on the secular clergy of monasticism's leap into the future.

So it is clear then that Catholic structures of governance have always tended to reflect rather closely their cultural milieu. When European society was feudal, so was the Church. When society became monarchical, so did the Church. But, Catholic structure has also avoided total imitation of the secular political forms surrounding it. In Roman times, bishops were elected, even though civil officials served at the whim of the emperor, himself usually a hereditary dictator. The process of selecting bishops in those times always involved an element of lay consultation. Even the stern John Chrysostom insists that the people participate in the decision (On the office of bishop, *De Sacerdotio, H, 4;* IV, 2). As another example, in theory the pope has the powers of an absolute monarch. But even in the days of absolutism the pope could not determine the choice of his own successor. The principle of election endured despite attempts to corrupt it through nepotism, bribery, and political manipulation.

Still, the concern of the Church not to be overly identified with any secular structure works both ways. Today, the democratic ideal in society seeks the greatest possible freedom and participation in decisions and in life by the people. The Catholic Church has taken much of that experience to itself. But it also remains convinced that even though civil society operates by majority rule, there is an element of administration in the Church's own life that is not subject to vote, but that has an unchanging quality under the guidance of the Holy Spirit.

For some 400 years, in response to both the Reformation and the rise of nationalism in Europe, the Catholic Church has been highly authoritarian and centralized. As the papacy suffered harsh criticism in the last century, the popes of that era struggled to reassert the authority of their office, especially through the declaration of papal infallibility in 1870. In retrospect, the latter action may not have done much to address the larger issues of the pope's role, since infallibility does not apply to matters of administration, but only to issues of doctrinal or moral theology.

A further result of Catholic defensiveness was the hierarchy's tendency to identify itself with the Church. The laity came to be viewed in a very restricted light. They were to be ministered to by the hierarchy—that is, by the "Church." The notion that the laity have a primary ministry to the world and to each other was severely attenuated.

Catholic Authority Today

Amazingly enough, the Catholic Church began to change all this, in fact to change itself, at the Second Vatican Council. Summoned by the beloved Pope John XXIII, the world's bishops met in a great reforming assembly that started to slough off the unnecessary and hampering cultural accretions of centuries. A new path was charted, or perhaps better, the bishops sought a return to the practice of former times, when lay ministry was more integrated with their own in consultation and collaboration.

It is quite accurate to say that in the years since Vatican II, the Catholic Church has undertaken a mammoth retooling of how it operates. The pope has established synods of bishops that meet every three years, restoring and regularizing the ancient tradition of church councils. In each country, a national conference of bishops operates with boards and committees that include clergy and lay alike. We see at the diocesan level pastoral councils, again with representation by the entire church community, along with strategic planning programs that include everyone. The parish has seen a proliferation of boards, committees, and other consultative bodies, some of them, like parish pastoral councils and finance committees, mandated by church law. And perhaps most significantly, ministries once closed to all but priests have now expanded to include literally thousands of lay people. The Catholic Church is entering a new phase that brings serious responsibility to all its members for its life and mission.

Since we view authority as a ministry of service designed to aid the Church's mission, the bishops continue to have a particular responsibility for leadership and for maintaining unity both in belief and in action. They are charged with the duty of teaching and preserving orthodox doctrine. They have a leading part in fostering and promoting Christian activities. At the same time, there is a wide area for initiative by individuals and voluntary groups in the Church. These do not operate counter to authority, but independently of it, far differently from the demanded and clear connection of the recent past.

Authority nonetheless does remain a very significant and strong element in Catholic life. For an older generation, their experience of authority was largely in the local parish, above all with the pastor, although other priests carried authority as well. Priests, and in some cases men and women religious, managed most parish institutions. But now the experience is far more diffuse, with a variety of people serving as parish administrators, school principals, directors of religious education, and in a host of other capacities.

In keeping with the renewed Catholic appreciation of the whole Church's ministry to the world, bishops and others in leadership positions recognize their responsibility to foster the development of lay spirituality. In the parish, but not there alone, we find opportunities for people to grow in the understanding of their Christian calling, even as they grow in faith and holiness. We have such things as Bible study groups, seminars in social teaching, forums on the relationship of faith and science, involvement in community organizing, and meetings of business people to discuss the ethics of their work. It is here, in such smaller groups both within and outside the traditional parish that most faith formation now occurs in Catholic life.

Another current emphasis is the need for authority to foster and guide Christian action in the secular world—the main arena of the Church's mission. The bishops seek to encourage and to support lay people in roles of leadership for secular society and in service to it. They attempt to bring the experience and tradition of the Church to bear on major social issues and to foster directions, caution consequences, or condemn particular movements in the light of moral values and perceptions of human dignity. There also remain large numbers of the laity who need to understand better how to integrate their faith and their work.

Since the central focus and highest activity of any Christian group is assembly for worship, the bishops continue to have a role in creating models of prayer and sacramental practice. In Catholic life, the Sunday eucharist in the parish plays an elemental part in everything the people do during the week. Other devotional practices will largely flow into or be inspired from it. The changes in both the language of liturgy and its structural forms since Vatican II represent authority seeking to be of service in this vital area for the mission of the Church.

It is quite true to say that the Roman Catholic Church has experienced an unprecedented degree of change in the religious lives of both clergy and laity since the Council. The situation continues today, and we still face many challenges. Perhaps the greatest of these is the development of shared responsibility and the adjustment to this approach in practice. We are leaving behind an era when the authority of bishops was heavily emphasized. Lay people in the Catholic Church are accustomed to being led more than to striking out on their own when it comes to the Church's mission. Clergy and laity alike are called to new forms of action and interaction.

Mikhail Gorbachev and others have noted that the effort to transform Russia into a political democracy is hampered by the fact that the Russian people have virtually no experience with the system. Something similar has been the case for the Catholic Church for many generations. We have the notions and procedures of consultation and group decision making rooted in our past. New processes can be learned, but for many they remain unfamiliar. Additionally, among our people, we have those actively resistant to change on the one hand, and on the other, in the words of one commentator, the "wildly revolutionary Christians." We continue to pray for the grace of the Holy Spirit as we move forward in this new and exciting era of growth. We are eager to learn from our brothers and sisters in other Christian traditions how better to make our own authority structures true servants of the Church's mission.

A Reformed Perspective

History
The Reformed tradition within Protestantism began almost immediately after Luther's break with Rome in 1521. It began in Switzerland with the work of Ulrich Zwingli and continued with many others, most notably

John Calvin. The setting of the sixteenth century, and particularly Switzerland in the sixteenth century, gave to the Reformed tradition a context of nationalism and at least limited forms of democracy. In the same way that the Roman Empire left its mark on the Roman Catholic Church, Swiss republican forms in a century dominated by nationalism have left their mark on the Reformed Churches.

From Switzerland, especially through the influence of the Genevan Academy, Reformed theology spread to many other areas. France, John Calvin's home before the necessity of exile, saw the growth of the French Reformed Church, called the Huguenots. Calvin had been forced to leave Geneva for a few years and during that time had been in the city of Strassburg. John Knox spent his exile in Calvin's Geneva, and when back in his native Scotland he developed the Presbyterian Church of Scotland, adding a variation of church government to what he found in Geneva. This Church was significant in the rise of Scottish national identity, opposed to English Anglicanism and French Catholicism.

In The Netherlands, the Dutch Reformed Church was strongly tied to the development of a Protestant country independent of Spain. When Mary Tudor took the throne of England in 1553 returning the country to Roman Catholicism, the Protestants who then left—the "Marian Exiles"—went to a variety of Protestant areas on the continent, including Geneva, Holland, and Strassburg. When they returned a few years later after Elizabeth became queen, many had been strongly influenced by the Reformed tradition. Out of this influence came the English Puritan and Separatist traditions.

Other parts of Europe had Reformed Churches: pre-Reformation Hussites in Bohemia and Waldensians in Italy became allied with the Reformed tradition; some small German states were also Reformed.

These Reformed Churches were independent of each other, united by similar theological understandings but not by any overarching form of government. Some of these Churches suffered enormously in the Thirty Years War and were almost totally destroyed. In France, there were rapid changes in the fortunes of the Huguenots due to policies of the crown. In England, attempts to force Anglican unity were opposed by the returned

Marian exiles, leading eventually to civil war. In Scotland, after the union of the crown with England, attempts to enforce Anglicanism there also met with great resistance. Because English colonies had begun in the New World by the time of these conflicts, many of the dissident groups came here, even French and German exiles. Dutch colonial efforts also added to the mix. This led to a great diversity of Reformed groups, but to a very strong Reformed presence in the United States, once the new country was formed.

The Presbyterian Church (USA) has major roots in Scottish, English, and Scotch-Irish immigration, as well as incorporating congregations that had French, Hungarian, Czech, and other origins. The Reformed Church in America has Dutch Reformed roots. The United Church of Christ includes largely English Congregationalist and German Reformed ancestry.

Basic Affirmations

In spite of the diversity and independence of Reformed Churches, there are several basic affirmations that underlie their understanding of authority in the church, including the role of laity in church decision making.

1. *Jesus Christ is the Head of the Church.*

This affirmation has several significant implications. First, because Jesus is a living Lord, present in the life of the Church, there can be no human being who takes his place. This lies behind the Reformed refusal to acknowledge the papacy. There can be no vicar of Christ. Second, no human governing body can claim absolute authority.

This leaves the Reformed tradition with the very real question of how Christ is to be understood as governing his Church in the present. Are there structures for this? The answer is both simple and complex. The simple answer is that Christ governs through his word and the Holy Spirit. The answer is complex as to how the word and Spirit are understood to function in the life of the Church.

2. *Holy Scriptures are the only rule of faith and practice in the Reformed Churches.*

The Word of God comes to us in Scripture. The authority of Scripture is derivative of the authority of Christ because Scripture witnesses to Jesus Christ. For this reason, all Christians are urged to read, to study, and to meditate prayerfully on Scripture. However, this does not require an individualistic interpretation of Scripture. The community of faith is the basic context for the individual Christian's interpretation of Scripture. This is seen in several ways.

- **The stress on preaching.** Preaching is the interpretation of a biblical text so that it becomes a living word, applied to the congregation gathered around the word. Implied in this is an awareness that the move from the ancient text to the contemporary situation is not always an easy one. Much of the Reformed tradition stresses the particular calling of those who do such preaching. The assumption is that God calls specific persons to this task. The role of the governing structures of the Church is to discover and to approve those it believes are so called. This approval is the major content of ordination. The public worship of the congregation, particularly on the Lord's Day, includes the proclamation of the word. The words of the sermon are human words based on the word of God, but, as put by Karl Barth, the Swiss Reformed theologian, God can take our human words and make them God's own word to the congregation.

- **The emphasis on education.** Within the life of the congregation, most churches assume that there will be a program of education, often carried out as Sunday school classes for children and adults, women's groups, or other forms. Traditionally, Bible study has been a significant part of that educational program.

- **The role of Confessions of faith.** Most of the Churches of the Reformed tradition have one or more confessions of faith that are accepted as the basic outline of the interpretation of Scripture. For English-speaking churches, historically, the *Westminster Confession* has been dominant. There is also the *Scots' Confession*, the *Second Helvetic Confession*, the *Belgic Confession*, the *Heidelberg Catechism*, as well as more contemporary ones. Since the highest authority is usually the national church, different churches hold different confessional standards, although all would be recognizable as "Reformed." These confessional standards usually must be accepted by officers of the church, both clergy and lay. Members who are not officers do not need to subscribe to these fairly elaborate theological statements.

The confessions of faith are an important way in which the historic tradition of the Church comes to bear upon the present. The confessions are understood to be agreed upon interpretations of Scripture and are always reformable by Scripture. They are authoritative but not infallible. Their adoption by any national church requires approval by various levels of the Church, all of which include elected laity as well as clergy.

Churches of the Reformed tradition that hold to a congregational form, where final authority rests in the congregation and not any structure above that level, do not have the same historic confessional forms. This would include the United Church of Christ.

Much of what has been said thus far about Christ governing the Church through the living word needs to be nuanced further. The rise of the scientific method and the Enlightenment in general raised serious issues for many Protestants of the Reformed tradition. At the end of the nineteenth and beginning of the twentieth centuries, many Reformed Churches in this country were torn between Modernists (or Liberals) and Fundamentalists (or Conservatives). While the Roman Catholic Church was developing the understanding of the infallibility of the bishop of Rome, Reformed Protestants were dealing with issues of the infallibility of Scripture. In the midst of the challenges of the modern world, there was the desire on the part of many to find an unquestioned authority that could withstand the onslaughts of modern science. The Fundamentalists held to the infallibility of Scripture, the inerrancy of its words.

Along with inerrancy there was often an assumption that the words of Scripture themselves needed little or no interpretation. There is a timelessness to the words, so application to the present is not a difficult matter. For some people, this made the task of preaching less important, since the individual Christian could read the text and make the application. This is a major source of the individualism that has come to dominate much of the contemporary Church.

In the past several decades, it has become clear that many within the Reformed tradition—especially younger people—have very little knowledge of Scripture and even less awareness of the Confessions of faith. Education about Scripture within the family, within the local congregation, and within the wider culture has diminished greatly. Where there is such biblical illiteracy, the Reformed understanding of the present rule of Christ as head of the Church obviously faces serious problems. The Church runs the danger of having individual preferences not based on Scripture become the authority within the life of the Church.

3. All human beings are sinful.
This includes Christians. Therefore, decisions central to the life of the Church ought not to be in the hands of one person. Every level of the life of the Church makes decisions by a process that includes those elected by the community of faith or by the whole congregation.

Reformed Christians have a great dislike of authoritarian rule, in the Church or in the wider society. Historically, they have disliked monarchy and have worked for democratic structures. Some in the Reformed tradition have preferred direct democracy, such as the Congregational churches or the New England town meeting. Most of the Reformed Churches have preferred representative forms in both ecclesiastical and civil life. In all cases, there are written constitutional forms that function as both canon law and theological definitions.

The fear of rule by one person lies behind the Reformed antipathy to episcopal forms. It is not only the bishop of Rome but all bishops who exercise rule by one and therefore can present great danger. One can interpret presbyteries or consistories as collective bishops, groups of clergy, and representative laity elected by congregations, who make the decisions usually made by bishops in episcopal polities.

4. There is reliance on the presence of the Holy Spirit.
This is true in the reading and understanding of Scripture, in the prepara-

tion and delivering of sermons, and in the gathering of those entrusted to make decisions for the life of the Church. That is to say, the Church cannot rely on its own ability to read and interpret Scripture or to make decisions. Christ acts in the Church by means of the Holy Spirit. Therefore, those who elect representatives cannot ask how they will vote on issues. The elected must be free to be influenced by the Spirit in the gathering where the decisions are to be made. Therefore, elections are to be based solely on the grounds of who gives evidence of faithfulness and a sincere desire to be open to the working of the Spirit.

Conclusion

The Church develops in the world and is influenced by it. The form of government within the Church is shaped at least in part by the political models available—the Roman Empire, the Swiss city state. The events of the wider world have influence within the life of the Church—the Enlightenment, the development of the modern world with all of its scientific methodologies, its stress on the individual. Neither Roman Catholic nor Reformed Churches have been able to create walls that keep out the world around them. Both Churches, in various ways, have tried to do so. But that is not the case in recent decades. There is always a need to evaluate the influence of the society around the Church, but it cannot be dismissed as a Godless reality. Nor can the Church remain unchanged as the situation around it alters. Christians live in the civil society as well as in the Church. This is particularly true of the laity who live out their Christian lives in the world, making decisions about what their faith calls them to do.

Both the Catholic and the Reformed Churches ultimately rely on the work of the Holy Spirit to make their institutional structures work. Both assume that the Spirit will guide them in the institutions in which they live. Increasingly, the Spirit seems to be moving us toward one another, as well as toward the world around us. Our traditions are influencing each other, as we both seek to understand what it means to be faithful in today's world. Walls are coming down, and instead of walls we are discovering permeable borders between Churches and between the church and the world. If this is the case, we need to look closely at what is happening in the world around us. What are Christian lay people already doing in the world because of their faith? The Church is a community that nutures the faithful, but the whole Church can learn from the experience of faithful lay people.

Discussion Questions

1. Is there any church organizational structure that could not be misused by human beings? Is there any church organizational structure that could not be used by the Holy Spirit?

2. In seeking to discover what God would have the Church do in a specific situation today, is a single individual or a representative group of the faithful more likely to discover the truth? Why? What are the dangers on either side? What are the strengths?

3. How does the whole Church learn from and evaluate what Christian lay people are doing on the basis of their faith in the world outside of the institutional church?

Chapter Three

EPIGRAPH

This section by far is the most creative aspect of this present Reformed/ Roman Catholic dialogue. We live today in a highly pluralistic world, but one that experiences profound distrusts and even animosities. How countries and ethnic groups come to grips with their hostilities, and at the same time their hopes for life in harmony, offers the Churches a unique process for their coming together, for their facing doubts, for their facing differing ways of seeing both Jesus and the Church and still learning to love each other. The committee urges you to read this carefully and to consider its powerful possibilities for a *koinonia* Church on the verge of a third millennium. Key to this process is the ability to understand and to realize compassionately that there are not impermeable boarders between Churches sharing the same faith in the Lord Jesus and professing the same creed in one Church, the one Lord, and the one baptism.

Chapter Three

PERMEABLE BOUNDARIES: LAY CHRISTIANS IN A CHANGING WORLD

by Bro. Jeffrey Gros, FSC (Catholic Perspective)
Mr. Harold H. Saunders (Reformed Perspective)

Catholic

. . . The Church, then, believes it can contribute much to humanizing the human family and its history through each of its members and its community as a whole.

Furthermore, the Catholic Church gladly values what other Christian Churches and ecclesial communities have contributed and are contributing cooperatively to the realization of this aim. Similarly, it is convinced that there is considerable and varied help that it can receive from the world in preparing the ground for the Gospel, both from individuals and from society as a whole, by their talents and activity (*Gaudium et Spes* [Vatican Council II, 1964], 40).

The Father has shown forth his mercy by reconciling the world to himself in Christ and by making peace for all things on earth and in heaven by the blood of Christ on the cross. The Son of God made man and lived among men in order to free them from the slavery of sin and to call them out of darkness into his wonderful light (*Praenotanda: Rite of Penance*, Paul VI).

Reformed

To be reconciled to God is to be sent into the world as his reconciling community. This community, the Church universal, is entrusted with God's message of reconciliation and shares his labor of healing the enmities which separate men from God and from each other. . . .

The Church, in its own life, is called to practice the forgiveness of enemies and to commend to the nations as practical politics the search for cooperation and peace. This search requires that the nations pursue fresh and responsible relations across every line of conflict, even at risk to national security, to reduce areas of strife and to broaden international understanding (*The Book of Confessions* [New York: United Presbyterian Church, Office of the General Assembly, 1980], p. 5).

We pray for the fruits of the Spirit of Christ
 who works for peace on earth,
 commands us to love our enemies
 and calls for patience among the nations.
We give thanks for God's work among governments,
 seeking to resolve disputes by means other than war,
 placing human kindness above national pride,
 replacing the curse of war with international self-control.
We hear the Spirit's call to love one another
 opposing discrimination of race or sex,
 inviting us to accept one another,
 and to share at every level
  in work and play,
  in church and state,
  in marriage and family,
 and so fulfill the love of Christ.

(*Our Song of Hope*, 1978 Reformed Church of America)

Preface

Christian laity have the capacity and the opportunity to lead in the movement toward church unity as it may appropriately be defined in the twenty-first century. The foundations for rethinking the character and role of the lay Christian must be built from fresh thinking about the nature of the changing world where the whole Church of Jesus Christ lives and works.

We start by placing our thoughts about the character and role of the laity in the context of the wider world and broad human experience. We begin with this world perspective because this is the setting in which the unity of the baptized must ultimately be realized and with which smaller communities of believers must find harmony. "Go, ye, into all the world. . . ." Then we proceed to examine today's political communities and Christian churches where Christians first form the relationships through which they work in national and international settings.

New insights emerge in each of these three arenas. These three will outline our consideration of "the lay Christian in a changing world" below.

- First, profound changes in how states, governments, and peoples interact in our increasingly interdependent post-Cold War world challenge traditional thinking about the capacity of states and governing authorities acting outside partnership with their own citizens.

- Second, as countries new and old seek to build, strengthen, adapt, or rejuvenate civil societies and participatory polities, fresh perspectives on politics within states enlarge political capacity among citizens outside government.

- Third, Christians within and across political boundaries are jarred by these changes and help shape them. They take this experience into their churches where they further shape change in light of their experience within those churches.

In each of these arenas, the spotlight falls afresh on the individual citizen—the individual Christian. In that perspective, our attention is drawn from the institutional to the human dimension of our lives together.

The mobilization of the whole People of God—the *laos*—is a critical dimension of answering God's call to restore the unity of the Church in mission, faith, witness, sacrament, and life. If we see the Christian community as a reconciler in the modern world, that community must be reconciled within itself. Millions of persons are called to the ministry of the Church. Some from among the *laos* are called to the special ministry of word and sacrament and are ordained to particular responsibility within the People of God. All, however, have the responsibility of bringing God's reconciling will to bear in a divided world, according to their calling in Christ.

This chapter defines profound conceptual shifts in how we look at the larger world around us, at the political lives of people within countries, and at the ecumenical movement. It is the laity who bridge all three worlds and struggle to find a coherence of new relationships among them. The Church is heavily invested in every dimension of life. The reader will find it helpful to consult the glossary to clarify some ideas in our two traditions.

Why should practical Christian people, who themselves face over-whelming pastoral and secular demands, spend time talking about "conceptual shifts"? Why should we discuss how countries relate, the nature of politics, or the nature and organization of the Church in such a document as this?

Experience teaches that the conceptual lenses we use to focus our under-standing of the world around us will determine how we act in that world. This chapter highlights the central role to be played by citizens outside government—including the Christian laity—in guiding our world and the Body of Christ through an era of profound change. The conceptual lenses Christians use to bring that secular world into focus will be the same lenses that determine how they take their faith into that world.

It makes a difference, for instance, whether we see the world through the lenses of competing Christian churches or through the lenses of a uniting Christian community. It makes a difference whether we see conflict as a contest of material power or as a creative tension among essential Christian values. It makes a difference whether we see the resolution of our differences in the Church as the work of ecclesial institutions and negotiators or whether we see it also as an act of reconciliation among baptized believers.

It also makes a difference when we see that concepts used to bring the secular world into focus have their direct counterparts in the ecumenical world. We speak of the total relationship among citizens across permeable national boundaries to pursue shared interests. At the same time, we have found need for the biblical word *koinonia*—communion, community, solidarity, fellowship—to capture the total pattern of interactions across permeable boundaries that divide the whole People of God.

Shifting our conceptual lenses opens the door to a vast untapped reservoir of Christian human resources for tackling problems in the ecumenical movement that heretofore seemed almost out of the reach of theologians and church leaders. It may open the door to new forms of power that can emerge from new relationships among people. This conceptual shift makes the role of the laity and of lay ecclesial organizations a priority— perhaps a prerequisite—in building the relationships necessary for a united Church.

Shifting our conceptual lenses also opens the door to the most human course to reconciliation—dialogue as contrasted to the formal tools of negotiation and mediation. We find that the capacity to relate at a human level through various forms of dialogue[1] is an essential building block toward reconciliation—one that is yet to be developed fully. We are gratified that this chapter is itself the product of such dialogue. We recognize that the Holy Spirit is present when Christians come together in honest dialogue, discerning God's truth, and his word for action in the world. Dialogue is the instrument of citizens outside government and, therefore, of the laity. Formal theological dialogue and institutional collaboration also have their appropriate contributions to make. Dialogue and shared action among the baptized can lead the way to unity.

We are asking lay Christians to think about how they are connected to the larger world each time they reach out to others. Acting in the name of Jesus Christ, they are a part of the People of God who are not defined by physical borders.

The Lay Christian in a Changing World

Rethinking How Countries Relate

We are living in the midst of a fundamental shift in our understanding of how the international world works. This is not a shift simply because the Cold War ended; it is rather a shift in the perspective of three and a half centuries of thinking about the nation-state system.[2] The changes that make bodies politic more interdependent have been maturing steadily under the frozen surface of the Cold War, but the reality has run well ahead of the conceptualization of that reality.

The Body of Christ has played and is playing a pervasive role in that shift—spiritually, conceptually, and politically—in those parts of the world where Christian believers are at work. Because it is essential to be concrete in placing the Christian laity in that larger context, we begin with three observations about our changing world.

First, governments of nation-states increasingly face problems that no one of them can deal with outside relationships with other partners. Those partners include other governments. Even at the height of the Cold War, the governments of the Soviet Union and the United States learned that neither could enhance security in a nuclear world without cooperating with its adversary. Governments acting alone cannot deal with problems of the larger environment, with disease, or with a global economy. But increasingly, governments are also realizing that many problems are beyond their reach unless they develop new partnerships with their own citizens.

Second, citizens outside government—working through public associations they create—increasingly participate in the conduct of politics and international relationships. What citizens acting in new relationships with each other did in East Central Europe in 1989 helped end an empire.

Citizens acting together in Latin America at the same time brought nations out from under authoritarian rule. People working together have forced change in South Africa. The Christian community and ecumenical common witness have contributed to this process.

Many of the conflicts that preoccupy the world today have flared out of the needs of human beings—out of clashes of human identity, grievance, fear, and hatred. These conflicts sometimes seem beyond the reach of governments. Nongovernmental organizations are increasingly stepping in to do what governments alone often cannot do.

Third, the traditional concepts of international relations—state, power, national interests—are not broadly enough defined to describe how the world works today; the traditional instruments of statecraft—military force, economic power, propaganda, and negotiation—do not reliably produce the results expected of them.

As United Nations Secretary-General Boutros Boutros Ghali wrote in 1992 of the state: "The foundation-stone of [building peace] is and must remain the State. . . . The time of absolute and exclusive sovereignty, however, has passed; its theory was never matched by reality."[3] In Bucharest, Budapest, Prague, and Berlin in 1989, as well as in Poland over a longer period, those who held raw power were dismissed by those armed only with the political power they themselves created. Interests are defined not only analytically in government offices but also by people in the political arena; they are defined politically to reflect what people care about and need as well as objective requirements of the state.

Among the instruments of state, the United States in Vietnam, the Soviet Union in Afghanistan, and Israel as well as the United States in Lebanon, for example, all learned that military forces are not equipped to restructure political life or even to sustain governments that do not have broad popular support. The Arab-Israeli peace process has not been negotiation alone but a series of negotiations embedded in larger political processes that have gradually changed individuals' perceptions and relationships.

We claim no originality for these observations; each reader could develop a comparable list. Unlike others, however, we do suggest that these observations require a fundamental change in thinking about how countries relate.

The traditional state-centered way of looking at the world could be put like this: Leaders of nation-states amass economic and military power to pursue objectively defined interests against other nation-states in a zero-sum contest of material power. This is often referred to as the "power politics model." The metaphor often used to capture this view was the strategic chess game.

An emerging view that more accurately describes our changing world can be stated in a formulation such as this: *Relationships between countries are increasingly a political process of continuous interaction among significant elements of whole bodies politic across permeable borders. To capture that political process of continuous interaction going on simultaneously at many levels, it is necessary to focus on the dynamics of the total relationship—the overall pattern of interactions. We have chosen the word* relationship *to denote this process.*

Governments continue to be major actors, and the nation-state remains the primary unit of organization in international life. But more and more often, governments increasingly discover that they are only one actor among many because other elements of the bodies politic of which they are part increasingly influence or actually carry out the conduct of international relationships. Governments are discovering their need for a new partnership with citizens outside government who claim responsibility for their own future.

As significant elements of whole bodies politic interact using the modern technologies of communication and transportation, governments are less and less able to control what crosses borders once considered exclusive boundaries of a sovereign state. Increasingly since the Helsinki Final Act was signed in 1975, the world community has considered gross human rights violations within a state the proper concern of all humankind. The relationship between a government and its people that was once considered a government's exclusive preserve has become the legitimate concern of other governments and international organizations. To say this is not to deny the continuing need for a principle of international practice and law that forbids unjustified interference in a state's internal affairs. But what is justified is being redefined. The so-called sovereignty of the state is being rethought to preserve what is essential but to take account of increasing interdependence among peoples.

Why is this material on international developments important to the lay Christian? *Relationship* is a theological and human word, rather than a technical or political one. It captures the complexity, humanity, and dynamism of this simultaneous interaction among human beings and groups on many levels and across permeable boundaries. A human word rather than a legal or academic word is critical because this choice of vocabulary moves thinking about international relationships from a state-centered focus to a focus on the interaction of groups of human beings. As will be noted below, this relationship among all human beings is mirrored in the community to which Christians are called in the Church. Likewise, by its very nature as sign, foretaste, and sacrament of the Kingdom of God, the Church is called to serve the reconciliation of all Christians.

The message to those who study and teach international affairs is that their study is no longer the sole province of a political science, law, or economics focusing on material power; it is also the province of psychologists, anthropologists, theologians, historians, and others who focus on human beings.

For those who practice the conduct of international relationships, the message is that they must give as much attention to the human dimensions of conflict and the constructive conduct of international relationships as they do to the institutional and governmental. Political strategy may be even more basic than military, negotiating, or economic strategy.

For Christians, the message is that lay persons and organizations can have a significant impact on the conduct of international relationships. That is no longer the exclusive province of the institutional Church.

If one focuses on the interactions among groups of human beings, it is not enough to think only of resolving differences among those groups by

45

negotiation. Mediation and negotiation will remain important instruments for resolving conflict in human affairs. But in today's ethnic and racial conflicts, for instance, people are not ready to negotiate because people do not negotiate their identity, fear, historical grievances, misperceptions, and hatred. Only fundamental changes in relationships can deal with these human feelings.

In this changing world, the instrument for transforming destructive relationships is not just mediation or negotiation; the instrument is dialogue. In dialogue, the focus is not only the technically defined issues that lawyers and diplomats negotiate over; the focus is the total relationship. In dialogue, important words in a process of changing human relationships also include *sensitivity, compassion, love, caring, pain, common ground, deliberation, forgiveness, feeling, "we"* rather than *"they."* Genuine dialogue by its very nature is a process of building, deepening, changing relationships. It is a means of exploring the mystery of the human person and of understanding different others. One might even say that dialogue is one of the holiest moments a human being can experience.

Some criticize dialogue as "soft." There is nothing soft about bringing people who dehumanize, demonize, and kill each other together to talk through their fears, hatreds, stereotypes, and their hard-shared interest in ending bloodshed, tragedy, and tears. Dialogue itself is an essential element in Christian formation.

The challenge to change destructive relationships in the world is central to the Christian calling. It is not different from Christ's call to bring unity to the Church, nor less taxing than the relational commitment and skills needed to reconcile Christian divisions.

In short, an accurate conceptual framework for understanding how countries relate in our changing world opens the door to—indeed demands—the active, sensitive, insightful participation not only of Christian institutions as institutions but of individual Christians as well. If dialogue is the method and the overall relationship between groups of human beings is the focus, the door is open to lay persons as well as to organized churches to play as much of a role in the conduct of international relationships and the resolution of conflict as it is open to their governments.[4]

As that door opens to the involvement of citizens outside government in relationships beyond national borders, the importance of dialogue—the citizen's counterpart to official diplomacy—increases. Dialogue is central to every human relationship.

Life within Bodies Politic

Two threads of thinking about democracy have woven through Western democratic thought. They have taken different forms in different ages and places. In some eras, one has prevailed; in others, people have been more conscious of the alternative; but throughout the history of Western civilization, the two have lived side by side. At best, they should work in close partnership.

In the Secular Order

The more familiar thread of political thought for us has been our institutions and practices of elections, one citizen/one vote, representative government, majority rule, checks and balances to curb the power of government and to protect individual rights. It is the form of democratic practice enshrined in the Constitution of the United States, and it is what U.S. citizens—and many others around the world—think of when they think about "politics" or "democracy." It relies on those institutions to deal with a society where citizens' interests are normally in conflict, where large societies must be governed, and where the political system is akin to a legal system in which the adversarial proceeding is often thought to be the best method of getting at the truth.

The other way of picturing the practice of democracy is to go back to the Greek and Roman forums, to the New England town meeting, to the workings of many of the "associations" to which de Tocqueville referred, or to the workings of many community groups in today's United States. Instead of simply voting, people sit down in dialogue until they find the best way of dealing with the problems they face—often without waiting for government to address those problems. The emphasis is on finding shared interests underlying legitimate differences on which to base common approaches. The method is face-to-face dialogue rather than confrontation. The aim is to probe and to experience the dynamics of the relationships which must be changed in order for people to work together in dealing with their problems.[5]

In the Church

The biblical doctrine of the Church—its lived experience in history—likewise shares similar trends. We see in both the Hebrew Scriptures and the New Testament emphases on a variety of ways of ordering communities with definable borders and an institutional order, emphasizing leadership under God's will and Christ's revelation. We also see an emphasis on the responsibility and participation of all God's people, linked in the New Testament by baptism and the Lord's Supper. As in society, so in the Church, order is seen in the context of the full communion of the faithful. Conceptually, these two dimensions of Church are best understood in partnership.

The process of building the unity of the Church can be seen from these two standpoints. If one begins from the institutions that embody the Church's faith and structures, we might expect mergers more characteristic of secular corporations On the other hand, the unity of the Church can be envisioned from the conceptual standpoint of a set of relationships rooted in common sacramental life, common faith, and bonds of accountability and communion—all oriented toward a common mission in the world. While full agreement and unity must rest on deeper levels of agreement than now exist, relationships among Christians create the communion on which agreements and institutional renewal can flourish. Reception of theological agreement rests on their theological truth, but also on the trust and relationships that have developed in the receiving Christian community.

The Role of the Person

Each of these threads of thinking about the practice of community embodies a different view of the role of the individual citizen. Again, the two are complementary, not mutually exclusive.

In Society

Often accompanying the first view of democratic politics has been a concept of citizenship that emphasizes fulfilling legal obligations such as paying taxes, obeying laws, and exercising the right to vote. Going beyond that basic, somewhat mechanical view has been a concept—essential to the second approach—of the citizen as a political actor. The citizen is one who also claims personal responsibility for changing the environment in which he or she lives where that is necessary to deal with problems. It is a concept of the citizen joining with others in the give-and-take of dialogue and political exchange in order to change the relationships they must change to transform the course of their lives.[6]

The revival of this view of the citizen as political actor is rapidly gaining momentum as citizens in many parts of the world are voicing disillusionment with both newfound and established democratic machinery. Research shows U.S. citizens as angry at their exclusion from the political process by what they call a professional political class that, citizens feel, ignores their views once elected or appointed to office. Those citizens are voting less but working more in communities where they can make a difference.[7] Similarly, in countries like Chile and Argentina, citizens voted democratic governments into office and are distressed that those governments are not solving their problems. Organizations are growing up to provide citizens with experiences in deliberative and participatory democracy and with a sense that even democratically elected governments cannot work without active citizens as partners.

Coupled with this second view of democratic practice and citizenship is a distinctive view of authority—that sovereignty in human society rests in citizens themselves acting to constitute themselves as a body politic with governing structures of their own design. In this view, one thing that government cannot do is to create its own legitimacy; that can only be created by people acting in relationship with each other. Related has been a basic distrust of government and skepticism of its ability to deal effectively with problems when acting alone.

In the recent history of the United States, this second approach to secular democratic society was nourished by, among others, the Southern Christian Leadership Conference, which in the early 1960s ran a citizenship school at Dorchester, Georgia. Individuals from the rural South were brought into this school to understand what it means to be a citizen of the United States and what their powers as a citizen are. Individuals left those schools to teach others, and from that impetus came the voter registration drives and many of the sit-ins that became the hallmarks of the civil rights movement. In the late 1960s, a younger generation rebelled against the establishment and, in part, turned to communal organizations that paid more attention to the human basis of governance and to consensus-building as more appropriate forms of politics. The women's movement not only emphasized the equality of women but focused on a form of political activity that emphasized building, nurturing, and changing relationships through face-to-face dialogue rather than on accomplishing objectives through the use of power and confrontation.

These changes have led many in the United States today to recognize that the existing system of confrontational party politics, active interest groups and lobbyists, and a media that highlight confrontation no longer fulfill their expectations of what politics should be. No one would throw away the structure of institutional politics, but many believe it is not enough by itself. Many focus on "community politics" and what can be done by citizens in communities when they organize themselves to deal with their problems. The aim of those who work to enhance experiences in deliberative democracy is to build an alternative to "politics as usual." Other changes in society have provided a larger context for these shifts in democratic thought and practice.

In the Church
In the context of the church, the first approach leads to a sense of duty about attending worship, serving the organization of the church, financially supporting its mission efforts, and viewing the church as a source of personal spiritual nourishment. This view recognizes the priesthood of all believers, entered into by baptism, but leaves responsibility to church professionals. The second approach corresponds more nearly with the view of the Christian citizen as one who joyfully carries faith into everyday life and acts as a citizen claiming responsibility in the body politic out of a sense of Christian commitment and enthusiasm. In this view, the baptized Christian takes full responsibility for leadership in the Church, according to her or his gifts and calling. At the same time, the Christian citizen will bring into the Church some of the same questions about authority that pervade life outside the Church's walls.

Our thinking about the role of the lay Christian in the body politic beyond the doors of the church must develop in this context of a new emphasis on citizens claiming responsibility for changing their environments and the course of events, working in associations and communities to that end, and seeking a new relationship with government. Within the Church, a greater emphasis on community, lay participation, and bonds among divided Christians signals a renewal of the biblical understanding of the People of God, and the communion of local churches within a Church understood as universal.

The Churches in a Changing World

Contemporary thinking about the role and capacity of the leadership of organized churches has also been evolving steadily through this century. Questions increasingly have been raised about its ability to cope with our changing world, and increased attention has been given to the role of lay Christians in meeting those challenges. The history of the ecumenical movement could be written in terms of the institutional churches responding to lay initiatives.

This shift in thinking about the institutional Church and its relationship to all who are baptized has taken place alongside but not necessarily because of the shifts in the secular world. Beneath centuries of division have developed other complex links of interdependence. For 1,000 years the churches of East and West—and for 400 years Catholic and Protestant in the West—have seen themselves as exclusive of one another. At the same time, we claim never to have fully lost communion with one another in that we have acknowledged one another's use of the Scriptures, the historical creeds, the pastoral care provided for our people, and the sacrament of baptism. By the mid-twentieth century, the ecumenical movement represented a new reality in the theology of the Church (ecclesiology), in the experience of Christians and their identity, and in the conduct of the lives of the churches as institutions.

Lay Christians in different churches have increasingly developed relationships with each other to deal with problems that seemed beyond the reach of the organized church. In the twentieth century, the experience of lay Christians has led them to conclude that divided and exclusive churches do not respond adequately to the challenges of today's world or to God's will for the Church.

Several experiences of major lay groups have given rise to this change in perspective. Some of the more significant instances of lay people moving ahead were the following:

- The Sunday school movement of the nineteenth century in the British Isles and in the United States as well as social ministries in communities began to bring laity together.

- The modern mission movement, after 1910, learned that a witness to one Christ was undermined when preached to prospective Christians by openly competing missionary groups.

- The theological community recognized that common research—biblical, liturgical, and historical—was unearthing more common ground than previously realized.

- Sensitive Christians in the churches increasingly saw that divisions among them were incompatible with the Gospel of Jesus Christ on ethical, social witness, sacramental, and historical grounds.

- One of the more profound changes is the interchurch family, in which Christians both remain deeply committed to their still separate churches, yet live and work for the reconciliation of these churches, witnessing in their family and community to the real communion that can exist.

- Major social issues such as racism, poverty, multiculturalism, global violence, and feminism also brought Christians together across church lines.

- One can see all of these and other factors in the lives of "naturally" ecumenical Christian groupings such as the Focolari, base communities, and faith-sharing groups.

In short, it became clear to lay Christians living in a Christian, pluralistic environment that the religious debates of the eleventh to the sixteenth centuries were not theirs, no matter how deep the residue of those debates might lie in the faiths of the separated communities that nurtured them. The contemporary ecumenical movement has, in effect, brought an end to some religious wars but has only just begun to build the peace for which we search.

A Shift in How the Church Is Viewed

The gradual changes in thinking that have resulted from these experiences have amounted to the most fundamental shift in our understanding of the Church and its mission—the ecclesiology—that we have known in 400 years of thinking about our ecclesial identity following the Reformation. This is a paradigm shift. As churches absorb the many ramifications of this shift in thinking, it may be that the experience of the laity may well offer a significant path toward a reconciled Church. The traditional aim of common witness and theological exploration may not be large enough to take account of how the Church of Jesus Christ is working or is called to mission in today's world. Lay Christians are acting from the premise that they are *already* in real, if yet imperfect, communion.

The initial response in the early ecumenical discussions (1927–1952) showed church officials and theologians pursuing a methodology of "comparative ecclesiology," looking at our differences, comparing our doctrines and rituals, and clarifying mutual interpretations. This was an important trust-building phase for those who studied or experienced it. It was essentially an institutional response and an effort to negotiate toward formal mergers. Visible unity institutionally conceived was the goal.

The next stage has been one of "Christocentric methodology" (1952–early 1990s) in which scholars from different traditions working together have studied texts of Scripture and the developments of Christian history using modern tools of research, taking account of the identities of various communities in the contemporary context. Those engaged in this work addressed one set of resources and methodologies with a commitment to laying the grounds for a reconciled Church. This approach to church unity presumed God's will for unity, Christ's gift of unity by grace and revelation, and the Holy Spirit's presence in the common search for unity. All of these spiritual realities were, indeed, part of the vision of each Church prior to the ecumenical movement of our century. However, in these churches Christ's gift of unity, the presence of the Spirit, and the search for unity were seen through lenses of each separate church.

A new shift is taking place—namely, a shift that comes about by conversion of individual and church, setting aside negotiated approaches to

53
T

merger and allowing the Spirit to transform us and our institutions through open dialogue with the other Christian individual and church.[8] Building on the convergence unearthed by the theologians and the history of relationships, Christians work with one mind and heart to realize in their personal and institutional lives the unity in sacramental, faith, and church life for all Christian believers.

Another method holds that doctrinal issues should be set aside: "Action unites, doctrine divides." However, this practical and activist distinction neglects to recognize the fact that the People of God are driven to action in the world by their faith, and that decisions about Christian action can be as divisive as doctrinal formulations.

This work proceeds with the recognition that Christians in the world have already worked together in many ways regardless of denomination. Essentially, Christians discover that the issues of Christian faith and the order of the Church can only be resolved by common study of Scripture and of the heritage of the Church in the context of contemporary challenges. They feel that the new issues posed by the changing world must be addressed together in common mission and witness based on their common commitment to Christ and to reconciliation of the faith and sacramental life within the Church.

Lay Leadership
In many sectors of church life, the experience of lay Christians already far outstrips what church leadership is able to accomplish or what theologians are able to articulate. One problem that emerged is that theological ecumenical research over twenty-five to fifty years has been so fruitful that there is too much to be assimilated. Church leaders are faced not only with such conflicting forces in the world but also in their own communions and in the ecumenical movement that they sometimes seem almost paralyzed. Others feel we have moved too fast.

Christians hold that the relationships between churches are rooted in relationships between the whole People of God, whose baptism and confession of Jesus Christ already provide a level of communion yet to be achieved among our still divided churches. Baptism into the Church of Jesus Christ, this view holds, affects the entire life of a Christian. By sharing a common baptism, we are impelled to a hunger for common communion at the Lord's Table that is not yet possible. This sharing of the sacrament of the Lord's Supper is such a profound act for some Christians that it cannot be entered into until there is a higher degree of communion in faith and relationship to warrant such a deep communion, even though our common baptism cries out for eucharistic sharing (see 1 Cor 11).

As a Christian, the baptized person lives both within the church community and in the secular community beyond the Church's walls. The baptized person fulfills her or his mission in both communities. In this approach, the three dimensions of ecumenism—lay (social, spiritual, and pastoral), theological, and ecclesiastical (institutional)—are seen as complementary, not as separate or competitive.

At times, some theologians, particularly Roman Catholic theologians, have emphasized the baptized Christian's role only in the secular sphere, leaving the intrachurch sphere as the mission of the cleric. At times, other theologians and thinkers, particularly in the United States, have so emphasized the separation of church and state that one's religion is portrayed as "out of bounds" whenever a baptized Christian attempts to bring religious values to an area beyond the merely private area of one's personal life, or beyond the specifically ecclesiastical area of one's church life.

A formulation that may well describe the churches in the ecumenical movement, particularly in the laity's experience in the United States, is the following: *Relationships among churches are increasingly an ecumenical process of continuous interaction among whole bodies of believers, lay and ordained, across permeable borders.* The real, but imperfect, communion realized in baptism becomes incarnate in the relationships among Christian believers.

While the free movement of people from one church to another, whether permanent or occasional, may represent to some a certain shallowness of commitment, it may also signal a level of deep communion on which both understanding and ecclesiastical mutuality can be built. This is an ecclesial process among all of the baptized, which is a Christian human process of continuous interaction—not a linear series of decisions and ideas—at many levels, representing significant parts of the whole People of God across boundaries that ecclesiastical identities no longer fully control.

In this context, church leaders—if they are sensitive to their people and to the world in which they live—are discovering that they are only one element in the ecumenical process of reconciliation and the activities of the Christian community in the world.

While the purpose here is to focus on the unity of the Christian Church, we also keep in mind the wider human community. In the attempts to resolve larger issues in society, not only is there need for Christian to move with Christian beyond church lines, a dialogue between religions is also essential in our interdependent world.

The Biblical View of the Church

The biblical word we have begun to use in the ecumenical movement to capture this total pattern of interactions between the whole People of God is *koinonia*—communion, community, solidarity, fellowship. This communion is grounded in a deep-rooted shared conviction and sacramental reality. For the Christian, the relationship of the three persons of the triune God, distinct yet coequal, is the foundation for all life and relationships within the Church and with the world.

Christians have come to identify, together, certain structural elements that would be needed for full communion: (1) common confession of the Apostolic Faith; (2) mutual recognition of baptism, the Lord's Supper, and the ordained ministry; (3) common bonds of accountability and decision making; and (4) common mission in the world.

It must always be remembered, however, that the ecumenical vision of the unity of the Body of Christ is one of *relationship*, not merely of institutional structures. According to this vision, although the ecumenical initiatives developed by institutional structures serve the unity of the Body of Christ, that unity is manifested—indeed often appears first—in the relationship among lay Christians as they share their faith and work in sustained dialogue. *Koinonia* is a relational word used to speak of the relationships of the three persons in the one God—a word that implies shared faith, sacramental life, and witness to the world.

An essential element of the catholicity of the Church is the diversity and universality of different cultures. Throughout the world, Christianity is expressed in different ways. While we are speaking of the unity of the Christian Church here, we realize that interaction with the other religions of the world also is a part of the Christian mandate. It is by the mutual understanding and richness of this diversity, in Christ, that relationships between the variety of Christian people become one *koinonia*. This process builds on the relationships among individuals, congregations, cultural groups, and Christians in different nations. The unity of the Body of Christ is impossible unless there is an enabling process for people from divided churches to find relationships that bring healing to the Body of Christ and common witness in a polarized world.

Christians will do well to examine whether we see the world through the lenses of competing or complacent Christian Churches or through the lenses of a uniting Christian community. We need to analyze whether we see conflict as a contest of power or as a creative tension among essential Christian values. We are called to reflect on whether we see the resolution of our differences in the Church as the work of ecclesial institutions and negotiators or whether we see it as an act of reconciliation among baptized believers. The quest for the unity of the Church is God's work, to which we as believers are called to be accountable.

A Call for Dialogue and Lay Leadership

The lay Christian is a whole human being who lives at once in a changing world, in changing bodies politic, and in changing institutional Churches. This Christian cannot respond to these challenges of change, except by integrating his or her role as Christian and as citizen of the country and the world. Just as Christians see the need for the state to organize national and international life, we may see the continuing need for the institutional Churches to help organize the religious dimension of life. At the same time, citizens and lay Christians may find fulfillment through associations that cut across many jurisdictional borders. It may be that the religious identity of many is becoming simply that of baptized Christian.

The differences among Christians, where they remain divisive, are not differences that can be resolved solely by mediation or negotiation; they are differences that stem from deep-rooted human concerns—identity, fear, historical grievances, fidelity to beliefs, misperceptions, and misconceived hatred. Christian differences in faith and church cannot be solved by theology alone, though theology must address these problems. These differences represent profound parts of human life that cannot be formally and rationally negotiated. Only fundamental changes in relationships—human, theological, ecclesiastical—can deal with them.

That is why the final recommendation of this report is a continuing process of dialogue among lay Christians across the boundaries of our still divided churches. A guide to such dialogue appears later in this book (see "Five-Stage Process of Dialogue" in Part Two).

A process of dialogue has the potential to bring to the surface levels of trust consistent with our common baptism and profession of Christ; to generate experience in collaboration and common witness in areas where we do not feel constrained by denominational membership; and to create trust. Such dialogue can establish common ground; identify remaining differences; and provide a context for finding human, pastoral, theological, and ecclesiastical ways of dealing with these differences.

This is a call for the realization that the ministry of reconciliation among the whole People of God is central. It is as important as the technical theological task of clearing away the divisions of centuries or the serious institutional task of reforming church structure and practice.

The laity can lead. They can provide the spiritual, missionary, and communitarian openness and experience that create leadership and receptivity for reconciliation. The laity can engage actively through evaluation of the theological proposals for unity by studying and proposing creatively stages to concrete structures of unity.

The laity can lead. They can provide the spiritual openness and practical experience that generate both a drive and a receptivity toward reconciliation. The laity can design the practices of common action and steps for translation of theological proposals into concrete relationships that express underlying unity. With prayer and shared commitment they can imagine ways of preserving what Christians from different traditions value while bringing down the walls excluding one another.

Notes

1 Since this dialogue was completed, "*Ut Unum Sint:* On Commitment to Ecumenism," *Origins*, 25:4 (June 8, 1995): 49–72, was published. It will provide useful collateral reading to this text.

2 The standardization of the state system in Europe is generally dated from 1648 when the Peace of Westphalia ended the Thirty Years' War.

3 Boutros Boutros-Ghali, *An Agenda for Peace: Preventive Diplomacy, Peacemaking and Peacekeeping*, Report of the Secretary-General pursuant to the statement adopted by the Summit Meeting of the Security Council on January 31, 1992 (New York: United Nations, 1992), para. 17.

4 This view of the world is spelled out more fully in Harold H. Saunders, "An Historic Challenge to Rethink How Nations Relate," ch. 1 in Vamik D. Volkan, Demetrios A. Julius, and Joseph V. Montville, eds., *The Psychodynamics of International Relationships, Volume 1: Concepts and Theories* (Lexington, Mass.: Lexington Books, 1990). The concept of relationship is developed in Harold H. Saunders, "The Concept of Relationship: A Perspective on the Future Between the United States and the Successor States to the Soviet Union," an occasional paper (Columbus, Ohio: Mershon Center, The Ohio State University, 1993). The process of sustained, systematic dialogue to change conflictual relationships was first laid out in Gennady I. Chufrin and Harold H. Saunders, "A Public Peace Process" (*Negotiation Journal*, April 1993). It is applied to the relationship between Reformed and Roman Catholic Christians later in this volume.

5 The two threads of democracy are described in Jane J. Mansbridge, *Beyond Adversary Democracy* (New York: Basic Books, Inc., 1980) pp. 3-22. The tradition of democracy as practiced in the town meeting and the view of politics that starts from citizens rather than from political institutions is described in David Mathews, *Politics for People: Finding a Responsible Public Voice* (Urbana/Chicago, Ill.: University of Illinois Press, 1994).

6 This view of citizenship has regained currency in the United States in the closing years of the twentieth century. It is developed, for instance, in a white paper by Harry Boyte, Benjamin Barber, Suzanne Morse, and Harold H. Saunders, "The New Citizenship" (Minneapolis, Minn.: The Humphrey Institute of the University of Minnesota, 1993). See also David Mathews, *Politics for People: Finding a Responsible Public Voice*, op. cit.

7 The Harwood Group, *Citizens and Politics: A View from Main Street America* (Dayton, Ohio: Kettering Foundation, 1991).

8 Groupe des Dombes, *For the Conversion of the Churches* (Geneva: World Council of Churches, 1993).

Part Two

RESOURCES FOR CONGREGATIONAL DIALOGUES

GLOSSARY OF TERMS

by Dr Dolores R. Leckey (Catholic Perspective)
Dr. Catherine Gunsalus Gonzalez (Reformed Perspective)

Introduction

Early in the discussions of this fifth round of the Presbyterian/Reformed—Roman Catholic Consultation, the value of a glossary was put forth. Our own struggles to understand what "ministry of the laity" conveyed to Catholics and to Protestants suggested that others—particularly lay men and women of our respective churches—could benefit from some elucidation of common terms that appear whenever dialogue among Christians occurs. Pope Paul VI (in *Ecclesiam Suam* [*The Paths of the Church*]) spoke of dialogue as "spiritual communication" and said that it must be marked by clear, understandable language. While intellectually we may agree with that, it is only too easy for our conversations to fall into obscure or even arcane ecclesiastical jargon. Perhaps the increasing professionalism of church workers is a factor. But our focus in these dialogues is mainly on the 99 percent of the church body: the laity who are immersed in worldly realities that are, however, at least occasionally, recognized as "charged with the grandeur of God" (Gerard Manley Hopkins). It is these laity, too, who can become conscious of their "ministry" or "mission" to live the gospel of justice, peace, and reconciliation in all the far reaches and recesses of the earth, bearers of the good news, as it were.

The reality is that Christian laity—that is, the members of the Church not in holy orders or in consecrated religious life—come to consciousness in different church settings—for example, in Roman Catholic churches, in Presbyterian churches, in other Reformed churches. But increasingly they encounter one another in the settings of their mission or their ministry: in the family, in the workplace, in the political arena, in the realm of public service. They are engaged in dialogues of life.

Still, as Samuel Beckett once said, "it is not enough to have lived; one has to talk about it." And to talk about it intelligently and with understanding, one has to realize that language follows life, not the reverse.

Premature dictionaries are of little value and are ultimately ignored. This glossary, incomplete as it is, and somewhat tentative, attempts to reflect the life experience of women and men who have embraced the Christian Way under the aegis of different churches, but who frequently find themselves on a common path, the path of what we may call discipleship—that is, a commitment to learning and to faithful action, following the Way of Jesus the Christ. To that end, the entries tend to be expansive rather than crisp and succinct, following more an encyclopedia style. We think it is important that as borders become more permeable, as walls between people continue to come down, literally and figuratively, Christian dialogue—direct, unadorned, simple, and sincere—becomes an imperative of discipleship.

Catholics and members of the Reformed Church in America will find familiar echoes in the other's descriptions of church life. The Church as "mother," for example, is terminology found in both bodies, evoking a way of belonging that is decidedly different from political membership. They will also discover differences—the meanings of ministry, for example—although in the Roman Catholic Church there is a definite evolution of meaning underway that may lead to greater convergence of definition in the future.

It is our hope that Catholic and Presbyterian/Reformed laity will find this glossary an instrument to transform the dialogues of life into dialogues of language, and in so doing deepen understanding and respect for one another and for our "mother churches." In this way, Christian laity may newly discover the Word made flesh and experiment with enfleshing the word in both the community of the church and the community of the world.

In the Reformed Tradition

The Reformed tradition uses some of the same terms that are used by Roman Catholics. However, the meanings are not always the same. Confusion can arise unless there is awareness of these differences. In addition, there are some terms that have long been used by the Catholic tradition that have recently been appropriated by Reformed Churches. This has occurred because the terms seem more appropriate for new dimensions of our life. But often there is a subtle shift in meaning when such a borrowing occurs. There are also terms central to the Reformed tradition that need to be explained.

Vocation

In the sixteenth century, beginning with Martin Luther and strongly supported by John Calvin, there was a rejection of the superiority of the religious or clerical vocation over other roles or occupations in society. Protestants saw no preference for celibacy over marriage, and therefore found no place for a religious community based on celibacy, thus ruling out monastic life. In terms of the clergy, they wished to end any stress on priestly elements not shared with all the faithful. The prophetic or proclamation tasks remained and were strengthened by the emphasis on preaching that was the major work of the clergy.

For Luther, one's vocation was the way in which one served the neighbor. Even the most menial task can be a vocation, as long as it is a means of serving the common good. He did not see monastic life as doing this. Ordained ministry indeed could be a vocation, but it was no higher than others. Calvin agreed with this, to some degree, but added a much stronger sense of interior call to one's vocation, rather than response to external need or existing social placement. One had a specific calling to be a doctor or a soldier or a civil official or minister. The common good was most impacted by civil magistrates, and therefore for Calvin that was the highest of all vocations.

What has happened in the Reformed tradition is that the earlier stress on the variety of vocations has continued, but the stress on inner calling has increasingly been limited to the ordained ministry. *Calling* is the obvious English equivalent of the Latin-based *vocation*, but the terms are not used in precisely the same way. The questions, "Do you have a sense of calling?" or "Do you believe you are called?" are basic questions asked of candidates for ordination. Students are asked time and again to describe their sense of call. Rarely are such questions asked about other occupations in the wider society, though asking if one has a sense of vocation would be understandable.

Though it is understood that there is a specific call to ordained ministry, in our society it may be difficult for many people in other work to see what they do as directly serving the common good, or as a vocation in the classic sense. Work may be a means of earning a living, but personal fulfillment or efforts for the common good may be what we do around the edges, away from work, or after retirement. This may be part of the reason that many lay persons in the Reformed tradition have a difficult time with the classic Protestant understanding of vocation. It may be noted that, whereas for Calvin, the lay role in civil government was seen as the highest vocation for a Christian, political office is now viewed very cynically by many in the tradition. Recovery of meaning for the term *vocation* in all its fullness or understanding its contemporary possibilities may be part of the task of clarifying the mission of the laity.

Structures of Government

Though churches of the Reformed tradition hold certain characteristics in common, there are varieties of forms of government within the tradition. Some are congregational in structure. In this case, the whole congregation has the final decision-making power regarding accepting members into the congregation, determining the standards and organization of the congregation, deciding who will be the pastor, and issues of property. The pastor is a member of the congregation. There may be an elected board that administers the life of the congregation, but the basic decisions are made by the whole congregation. Even though such congregations are independent, there may well be regional associations of such churches that have general oversight of ordination and joint mission.

Most churches of the Reformed tradition hold to representative democracy and strong connectional links. In these instances, the congregation elects lay persons to the governing body of the congregation. In Presbyterian forms, these persons are called *elders*. Elders are ordained to office by the pastor but are not considered clergy. The governing body of the congregation is responsible for receiving and disciplining members, ordering the worship life of the congregation, nurturing members through pastoral work, as well as educational programs. *Pastoral* in this sense means care for the flock that is the congregation, and is the specific responsibility of the governing body, not only of the ordained clergy who are usually referred to as *pastors*. The pastor is a member of the governing body and chairs it but is not a member of the congregation. Rather, the pastor is a member of the regional governing body, usually called a *presbytery* or *classis*. When such regional bodies gather to make decisions, the clergy are joined by equal numbers of the lay members of the congregational governing bodies—the elders. These regional bodies have many of the traditional powers of bishops—ordination of clergy, organization and general supervision of congregations. Clergy and elders from these regional bodies are elected in equal numbers to national assemblies for decision making at that level. Elders and clergy serving in these capacities have the same powers and authority. There are no committees or structures for decision making in which clergy are separated from the lay elders.

Traditionally, Reformed churches have had boards of deacons. These are lay persons, elected by the congregation and ordained or commissioned by the pastor. They generally have the task of carrying out the works of mercy and reconciliation in the congregation and beyond. However, the work of the deacons varies greatly from church to church. Reformed churches do not use the tradition of the threefold ministry, and therefore the office of deacon is never a stop toward ordination as clergy. It is always a lay office in a congregation.

The congregation is the basic unit in a Reformed ecclesiology. Beyond the use of the term *congregation* for those gathered in worship, the word has a technical meaning. The congregation is composed of those who have been baptized and who have made a public profession of faith, accepted by those empowered to receive members, either the whole congregation or the representative governing body of the congregation. There are recognized ways of transferring membership from one congregation to another. Those members are eligible to vote on congregational matters and to be elected to offices. If such persons cease to participate in the life of the church in spite of efforts to restore them, they can be removed from the list of active congregational members. There is also a list of baptized children who have not yet made a profession of faith, and who therefore do not vote.

The terms *elder*, *deacon*, and *congregation*, and their specific uses within the Reformed tradition, are important for understanding the role of the laity. Much of the mission and ministry of the Church is carried out by the local congregation, which is the basic unit for the mobilization of the

People of God, especially in the local community. Though the pastor has a significant role in this, the major ordering of such mission and ministry is in the hands of the laity.

Christian Development

For both laity and clergy, the ability to carry out the mission of the Church in the world—the ability to minister in the Church and beyond—depends upon being a faithful disciple of Jesus Christ. Such discipleship is an ongoing process, begun at baptism, but continuing to develop through one's whole life. In the past, such development would have been referred to as *discipleship*—or *piety*—by those in the Reformed tradition. In recent years, however, these terms have been felt to be inadequate. Piety has come to be associated with external religious practices rather than internal commitment. There is a new emphasis on growth and development in the faith—even for adults.

Many in the Reformed tradition have borrowed terms from the Catholic tradition in order to express this renewed stress on growth in discipleship. Two terms in particular have been borrowed.

The first is *formation*. It is used both for the development of Christians in general and for clergy in particular. In the case of Christians in general, there are programs for the creation of small groups for the intentional development of discipleship, as well as resources for individuals. In regard to clergy, the term has a new popularity in seminaries in order to describe the nonacademic side of preparation for ministry: attitudes, character, way of life. It is often phrased, "spiritual formation."

Spirituality is also a recent Reformed import from the Catholic vocabulary. Spirituality has to do with the interior life in relation to God. There may not be a major shift in content between the older, positive understanding of piety and the newer use of spirituality, except that there is more openness to elements that earlier might have been regarded as "too Catholic."

There is still some hesitation in regard to "spiritual directors." Often the role is equated with that of confessor, and rejected. At the same time, many within the Reformed tradition see the need for such directors. The therapeutic role of pastoral counselor, long established within Protestant churches, is not seen as appropriate for the task of developing a deeper spiritual life. For this reason, many Protestants are turning to Catholic spiritual directors to fill this need and, at the same time, there is a move to develop such skills within the Reformed community and compatible with its tradition.

In some quarters of the Reformed tradition, the term *spirituality* has been used to limit the proper role of the Church to a narrowly defined "religious" arena, not having to do with the social, political, economic realms of life. Where this has occurred, the term *spiritual* can be misunderstood in this rather gnostic direction, and therefore it can be rejected.

In the Catholic Tradition

Apostolate

The *apostolate* is a term that was used more in the immediate pre- and post-Vatican II years to denote the laity's role as the Church's presence in society. The Lay Apostolate took many forms and applied to individual and corporate action by the laity. In some cases, the apostolate meant individual commitment to Christian action (mission), with the bishop's blessing, and with the possibility of being joined by others. An example would be Catherine de Hueck Doherty's establishment of the first Friendship House for purposes of countering racism. One Friendship House gave birth to others in the United States and in Canada. Those centers were places where the poor were welcomed and where dialogue between people of different races was encouraged. After the Lay Congress in Rome in 1950, Pope Pius XII asked Catherine (also known as the Baronness or "the B") to live separately from her husband, Eddie Doherty. Friendship House became a lay association whose members (men and women) lived under promises of poverty, chastity, and obedience and is now known as Madonna House.

Other examples of the apostolate are the St. Vincent De Paul Society, whose members live the Vincentian spirit according to the vision of Frederick Ozanam, the lay founder of the society. The society cares for the needs of the poor and is based in parishes. The Grail Movement is another example of the apostolate. Women living together in community help single working women through participation in the arts, in catechetical work, and in a variety of other community-based experiences.

One of the most effective methods of the apostolate has been that which is called "observe, judge, act." Small groups of workers, students, or married couples meet regularly to discern what is needed in the immediate culture and how to bring Christian values into the immediate environment. Young Christian Workers might focus on the workplace; Young Christian Students on the school environment; and the Christian Family Movement on family life and the neighborhood civic sphere. This method has given birth to many forms of small Christian communities in Latin America.

Men and women who preferred not to join with others in the apostolate participated in this outreach of the Church through applying their personal piety to various situations in the environment. They might gather with others for spiritual retreats or for a review of the rule of life that they had chosen, but their enactment of the apostolate was personal, drawing little attention. Opus Dei is an example, although technically it is *more* than a lay group; it is a "premature" or transgeographic diocese.

A decade after the close of the Second Vatican Council, laity who were engaged in theological studies expressed resistance to the term *apostolate*, possibly because it was understood to be connected to the hierarchy (and ultimately under their direction), and possibly because the unfamiliar term *ministry* was experimentally being used in reference to laity and was perceived to create a more equal relationship between clergy and laity. In ecumenical meetings and conferences of Catholics and others concerned about strengthening the laity in their role vis-à-vis society, Protestants thought that *apostolate* was an apt term for what they hoped to accomplish. It had a distinctiveness, they said, that marked a particular vocation and mission for the lay members of the Church. Why, then, have Catholics been hearing the term differently? One reason may be that in a church where governance has traditionally been limited to the official ministers, to be "in ministry" is thought to be a way into autonomy, and it carries with it emotional motivation. In many Protestant churches where issues around governance have been solved (in theory if not in practice), a separate, Scripture-based, action type term is welcomed.

In the period since the Second Vatican Council, several lay apostolic movements stand out.

The Christian Life Communities—small groups of men and women—follow the path of Jesuit spirituality, that is, "faith formation." It is international in scope.

The Community of St. Egidio began in Rome in 1968, as a small group of young adults who gathered each evening for prayer. It has grown into a community of thousands, whose members care for the poor, are ecumenically committed, and demonstrate a charisma for peace making. The Community has been nominated twice for the Nobel Peace Prize.

The Focolare Movement, also Italian in origin, is found in many countries throughout the world. Their fundamental purpose is to live lives of unity, and thus to foster unity across denominational, racial, and national lines. The movement's foundress is a recipient of the Templeton Prize for religion.

Deacon

The *deacon* is a man who is ordained to either the transitional or permanent diaconate, which is, in fact, a clerical state. Because married men, as well as those who are single, may be ordained permanent deacons, they are often mislabeled "lay deacons." Deacons are *never* laymen.

There are at this writing (spring 1995) approximately 11,000 permanent deacons in the United States. They are, for the most part, self-supporting. Within the ecclesial meaning of ministry, they perform a number of needed tasks, including marriage preparation, wake services, witnessing marriages, baptisms, and in parishes without resident priests, they conduct Sunday Services (i.e., Service of the Word with the distribution of Holy Communion which has been previously consecrated). The deacon's primary call, however, is that of direct service.

Formation

Formation is a term increasingly used in place of education when the reference is spirituality. *Christifideles Laici* (John Paul II, *The Vocation and Mission of the Lay Faithful in the Church and in the World* [United States Catholic Conference, 1988]) speaks of the continual process of growth and maturation needed if the laity's life and mission is to bear fruit. We are told that there is a dialogue between God, who offers his gifts, and the person, who is to exercise responsibility, and in that dialogue is the possibility of a total and ongoing formation of the lay faithful. (*Note*: The "dialogue" that characterizes spiritual direction can be thought of as an aspect of the dialogue between the person and God, and as an aspect of formation.) The fundamental objective of the formation of the laity is an ever clearer discovery of one's vocation and the ever greater willingness to live it so as to fulfill one's mission, according *to Christfideles Laici*. Formation occurs from being members of the Church and citizens of human society. Therefore, one can say that spiritual formation is woven into human formation and into intellectual, psychological, emotional, and social development. The Second Vatican Council has invited all the lay faithful to a unity of life, and the many interrelated aspects of a totally integrated formation of the laity are situated within this unity. *Christifideles Laici* emphasizes the importance of doctrinal formation, including social doctrine, and the importance of human values. Quoting a document of the Council, *Christifideles Laici* states:

> [The lay faithful] should also hold in high esteem professional skill, family and civic spirit, and the virtues related to social behavior, namely, honesty, a spirit of justice, sincerity, courtesy, moral courage; without them there is no true Christian life (*Decree on the Apostolate of the Laity* [*Apostolicam Actuositatem*], 4).

All people—clergy and laity—are formed by God, from the first moment of conception. From the beginning, God's Spirit and the human spirit touch. Then the Church enters the process of formation, first through sacrament and later through preaching and teaching.

The family is generally believed to be the primary site for formation. Clearly, children are formed within the "domestic church"—their home.

But adults are formed there too, through the dynamic of interaction between husband and wife and they with their children. Many parents testify that their children are a means of their adult formation, as they are called to be the loving bearers of authority that children need.

Christifideles Laici cites other places of formation: small Christian communities, the parish, schools, movements, and associations. Noteworthy is the mention of the reciprocity of formation: "Possibilities of formation should be proposed to all, especially the poor, who can also be a source of formation to all" (1987 Synod of Bishops, *Propositio* 41). Such a statement recognizes that formation occurs in the context of relationship or friendship, and implies mutual influence. This is an important concept in any discussion of Christian laity, who move about in many different worlds associated with church and culture, and who represent the church *in the world* not *against the world* (cf. Vatican Council II, *Gaudium et Spes* [*The Church in the Modern World*]). The image of Christian presence in the world—a presence of peace, reconciliation, hope—is a key to understanding the heart of the Lay Apostolate.

Formation of Conscience

Formation of conscience is considered a lifelong task, beginning in the earliest years of childhood. According to the *Catechism of the Catholic Church*, "Prudent education teaches virtue; it prevents or cures fear, selfishness and pride, resentment arising from guilt, and feeling of complacency, born of human weakness and faults" (no. 1784).

Scripture, wise spiritual counsel, the data of human experience and reason, the teachings of the Church are all incorporated into the formation of conscience.

Lay Ministry

Lay ministry is a relatively new term in contemporary Catholic vocabulary. The most authoritative source of our terms and terminology, the documents of the Second Vatican Council, uses ministry only in relation to priesthood. Pastoral practice in the postconciliar years has influenced the enlargement of the term, however.

In 1980, the U.S. bishops approved a statement *Called and Gifted: The*

American Catholic Laity, in which they stated that baptism and confirmation empower all believers to share in some form of ministry. It was the first official statement linking laity to ministry. *Called and Gifted* delineated two kinds of lay ministry. The first kind was called "Christian service in the world." By that the U.S. bishops meant business ethics, economics, cultural development, political life, and social justice.

The bishops also spoke of a second kind of ministry, internal to church life, which they designated *ecclesial* ministry. They named the contributions of volunteers and part-time workers who serve on parish boards and boards of education, who assist with catechetics, and so forth. They mention the lay people who serve in the domestic and foreign missions. And finally they speak of the lay persons who have prepared for professional ministry in the Church, and those who work in public service domains (i.e., housing, education, and job development). An increased role for women in ministry was an expressed hope in the document.

Many parishes—and some dioceses—have "commissioning services" for lay ministers, which signal that those commissioned have been properly prepared and will undertake their ministry under the aegis of the Church.

The theological foundation for lay ministry has been strengthened in the apostolic exhortation *Christifideles Laici.* There we read: "The Pastors, therefore, ought to acknowledge and foster the ministries, the offices and roles of the lay faithful that find their foundation in the Sacraments of Baptism and Confirmation, indeed, for a good many of them, in the Sacrament of Matrimony" (CL 23). However, *Christifideles Laici* recalls that some of the Synod fathers were concerned about too indiscriminate use of the word *ministry* which, according *to Christifideles Laici,* can cause confusion by equating the common priesthood (of the laity) and the ministerial priesthood. This confusion, it claims, leads to lack of observance of ecclesiastical laws and norms, a tendency toward "clericalization" of the lay faithful and the risk of creating, in reality, an ecclesial structure of parallel service to that founded on the sacrament of orders.

A special commission was appointed by the Vatican to study the matter of ministry from theological, liturgical, juridical, and pastoral perspectives. Membership on the commission is unknown, and to date there is no report.

However, in April 1994, approval was granted for dioceses to permit girls and women to function as altar servers (following discussion and consultation with the episcopal conferences). Concern over appropriate liturgical ministries for women was believed to be a major factor in establishing the aforementioned commission. At the same time (in April 1994), the pope, at a meeting in Rome sponsored by the Sacred Congregation for Clergy, rejected the use of the term *pastoral* in reference to lay ministry. He said one problem is that as lay ministries have burgeoned, the language used to describe the laity's roles has at times been uncertain and confused. Terminology should not confuse baptismal priesthood shared by all the faithful with the ordained priesthood of the clergy. The pope emphasized that the ministries and services performed by lay people "are never exactly pastoral, not even when they replace certain actions and concerns of the pastor." Furthermore, he said that "to clarify and purify the language is becoming an urgent pastoral task, because behind the language there can be traps that are much more dangerous than is generally believed."

Finally, it should be noted that a special subcommittee of the bishops' Committee on the Laity (of the National Conference of Catholic Bishops) has been established to study and to guide the responsible development of *ecclesial* lay ministry. Ecclesial lay ministry refers to those lay men and women professionally prepared for specific roles of service and leadership in the Church.

Parish Council

There are two kinds of parish councils in contemporary Roman Catholic church life. The first, a *parish finance council*, is required by the Code of Canon Law. This council is to comprise those with expertise in financial matters. The other, a *parish pastoral council*, is recommended by the Code of Canon Law, not required. A diocesan bishop, however, may determine that every parish is to have a pastoral council—which would help set priorities for the parish. Both finance and pastoral councils are advisory with final authority resting with the pastor. However, "it is an ancient tradition in church law that those exercising executive power seek counsel from others before taking action" (*Code of Canon Law: A Text and Commentary*, James A. Coriden, Thomas J. Green, David E. Heintschel, Mahwah, N.J.: Paulist Press, 1984). This reflects concern for drawing in the wisdom of the community through which the spirit speaks.

Spirituality

In starkest terms *spirituality* refers to nonmaterial reality. Christian spirituality refines the starkness by describing spirituality as knowing and following Jesus Christ through the power of the Holy Spirit. There is, in fact, *one* Christian spirituality, and it is rooted in Jesus. In this imitation of Christ, spirituality is woven into the material fabric of life—incarnational spirituality. For most lay Catholics, the path to this knowledge is prayer, meditation, and contemplation; the sacraments, including matrimony; Sacred Scripture; the works of mercy and of justice, especially in encounters with the poor and dispossessed. Spirituality, then, is both the content and the process of life consciously lived in the Holy Spirit. Spiritual direction is a ministry of the Church to assist the person on an intentional spiritual path.

Catholic religious orders have identified different pathways for following Christ, as have popular devotions of different ethnic groups. Special mention must be made of devotion to Mary, the mother of Jesus. This *Marian devotion* crosses ethnic, economic, and class lines; in the late twentieth century Mary is especially important as an inspiration and mediator for all kinds of oppressed people.

The ecumenical movement itself has developed as a form of spirituality as it deepens understanding of numerous others and enlarges the desire for unity.

Spiritual Direction

Spiritual direction in Catholic practice is often associated with the Exercises of St. Ignatius of Loyola, whereby one meditates on prescribed scriptures, notes the movements within one's soul—especially those of desire—discerns what God's will is for one's life, and comes to know and love Jesus and to follow in his way as a disciple. The spiritual director listens to the person describe consolations (feelings of joy, insight, gratitude, peace, etc.) that arise from the meditations and desolation (confusion, fear, apathy, etc.) and helps discern what the meaning of the consolations and desolations might be. The director "companions" the person seeking God along the spiritual path. There is an assumption that clarity and commitment regarding one's mission will flow from Ignatian spiritual direction.

Spiritual direction also occurs outside of the Ignatian method. The director listens to the prayer experience and life development of the directee and offers insight and commentary on what is happening in the realm of spirit. The spiritual direction relationship is essentially an intentional one wherein both parties become attuned to listening to the Spirit's call.

In the past, spiritual direction was often associated with the sacrament of penance—that is, one went to confession (naming sins in their particularity) and also discussed the state of one's inner life, receiving guidance and encouragement. Now, sisters and brothers living the consecrated life offer spiritual direction—as do lay people—so there tends to be more of a separation between the two.

One of the responsibilities of the spiritual director is to pray for the person he or she is directing.

Vocation

Vocation is understood, historically, as a call from God to a particular state in life. In the past, several vocations were acknowledged: priesthood (for males); religious life (for males and females); marriage and the single life (for the laity). While these several vocations were informally acknowledged, the term was formally associated with priesthood and religious life, which, until the Second Vatican Council, had a more developed theology than marriage. More recently, Pope John Paul II's apostolic exhortation *Christifideles Laici* speaks of the prime and fundamental vocation of the lay faithful as that of holiness defined as the perfection of charity (love) (see CL 16). Within the lay state, we are told, there are varieties of this fundamental vocation, differing according to age, sex, and talents. "In the field of a 'commonly shared' lay vocation 'special' lay vocations flourish" (CL 56). Secular institutes are one form of specialized vocation where members profess evangelical counsels of poverty, chastity, and obedience through vows or promises, while fully maintaining one's lay state.

What we have here is the vocation to holiness exercised within the lay state, which takes its character from the secular environment.

More recently in pastoral practice and pastoral theology, we learn that lay people discover a vocation to ministry—that is, to the service of the People of God.

Some Joint Concluding Words

To reiterate: this glossary is merely a tool to encourage what can surely be a sacred conversation about how we—Catholics and members of the Reformed Churches—live our dailyness. It is not complete, just as the conversation or the dialogue is not complete.

Dialogue is a value in itself, because at its best it helps individuals and groups encounter the mystery of the human person and ultimately the mystery of God. One analogy familiar to lay men and women of both traditions is that of marriage. When we marry—whether we consider it a sacramental state as do Catholics, or a serious covenant as do some other Christians—we enter into a lifetime of dialogue. The purpose is not to "solve a problem" or "win a debate," but to encounter at ever deeper levels, the mystery of the other. And to that end, one could say the dialogue never ends. Nor does it "convert" the other into "sameness." People do remain their unique selves.

So, too, in the ecumenical dialogue, the partners are not "converted" to each other's views. Rather, the uniqueness of each is expanded even as the sharing of life and faith experiences grows between them. The dialogue and the encounters are a means of spiritual formation of the participants, as they (we) continue our eternal pilgrimage. Through the dialogue, we help one another "endure the beams of God's love," as William Blake suggested long ago.

FIVE-STAGE PROCESS OF DIALOGUE

by Mr. Harold H. Saunders

In many communities, baptized Christians from both Reformed and Roman Catholic Churches work side-by-side to improve the quality of life for all in the community. They work together through civic committees and associations and in their vocations to provide necessary services and nourishment for body and spirit. Sometimes, they do this simply as citizens without reference to spiritual commitment; sometimes, they state openly that they are working together as baptized Christians.

At the same time, the Churches from which they come keep their separate doctrinal and organizational identities. In some communities, those traditional differences may still leave a residual suspicion and alienation, sometimes mixed with ethnic stereotyping.

To strengthen the relationships among baptized Christians in their common service in Jesus Christ, in their communities and in the wider world, this paper offers an approach to overcoming obstacles to full sharing in that common work. It is offered with the deep conviction that strengthening relationships among the laity is a fundamental and leading step to unifying the People of God.

The approach is *sustained dialogue*—a human process for changing strained relationships. It permits groups to preserve and enrich their own identities while developing the mutual respect that enables them to work creatively with others who may be different. This approach requires a commitment to engage in dialogue over time, but it has been widely tested and found to provide a deep human experience.

Possible Uses of Dialogue

A systematic process of sustained dialogue could serve several possible functions within the larger movement toward *koinonia* among baptized Christians. These are not mutually exclusive. Their usefulness depends on the needs of particular situation. Some examples.

First—within congregations. A fundamental obstacle to progress toward Christian unity is often more deeply rooted than issues of doctrine and polity. It sometimes lies in the gulf between two kinds of persons: (1) those individuals whose identity is firmly tied to their particular definition of the Christian message, which they see as the only true interpretation and which depends on declaring all others outside the circle of the saved; and (2) those individuals who identify with what they see as the core of the Christian message and with the hope of a church united around that core and tolerating various ways of expressing it. This divide is captured by familiar pejorative words such as *conservative, fundamentalist, extremist, rightwing,* and *liberal.* This divide exists within congregations and organized churches. It characterizes some Protestant denominations.

Dialogue would not seem a likely instrument for bridging this gulf because dialogue depends on willingness to listen prayerfully to another's views and feelings. Some would judge that there is little capacity to listen to the other on either side of this gulf. But experience with ethnic and racial conflicts, with which this division has much in common, demonstrates that many human beings are disturbed by such gulfs and are willing to try finding a bridge. That is a judgment each group will have to make.

Second—between congregations. It is possible to identify the key issues that still divide Roman Catholic and Reformed—not to mention other Protestant denominations—and to develop dialogue between congregations across denominational lines on these issues. Some of these issues have been historically quite painful. They are worth recalling briefly but concretely because they represent the paired mutual fears and judgments that may still consciously or subconsciously affect relationships between the denominations.

Each side fears that its identity would be submerged in another body whose full character is at best not fully understood or at worst malignantly misperceived. The historic grievances and fears on both sides have real roots.

For much of U.S. history, tension between Roman Catholic and Reformed Churches grew out of the fact that the American establishment has been characterized and dominated by a social and political creed that has roots deep in the Reformed tradition—practice of congregational government and a polity where the "citizen" is both the source of sovereignty and a primary political actor. Even as late as the 1960 election, fear of an external centralized authority—the pope—was a serious factor in American political life. Roman Catholics were seen as building an exclusive society behind walls of a separate eucharist, resisting intermarriage, and insisting children from a mixed marriage be raised in the Catholic Church. Protestants tended to view Catholic adherence to papal authority as a symbolic threat to participatory democracy and as having the potential for "dual loyalty," making Catholics in their eyes something less than fully loyal Americans.

As Roman Catholics came into that polity as immigrants, their experience gave them reason to fear the continuation of nativist, anti-Immigrant bigotry fanned into flames by often vicious appeals to these Protestant concerns and fears. Catholics have experienced the same kinds of discrimination and second-class citizenship, in some circumstances, as other religious and racial groups—an exclusivism and resistance to their very presence. They have often felt that Protestant society was telling them that they could only "make it" economically and socially if they abandoned their religious system. "Just give up the pope," generations of Catholics felt they were being told, "and we (the Protestant majority) will allow you and your children to enjoy the full benefits of U.S. citizenship. But if you do not abandon your 'popery,' we will continue to withold from you and your children the full benefits of U.S. citizenship." They were excluded from the "best" neighborhoods, membership in social and business clubs, jobs, schools, and full-fledged acceptance. Their children were subject to proselytism in the "public" schools. These discriminatory phenomena persisted throughout the nineteenth and well into the twentieth century. Catholics thus sought to combine an enlarged patriotism with an enlarged loyalty to the Holy See.

In matters of faith and moral practice, these differences in polity have raised fundamental fears that touch close to the core of human identity. On the one hand, many early Protestants who came to America to escape highly centralized political and religious control embedded deep in the American soul a compelling fear of such authority and control. Even in the last half of the twentieth century, that fear lay at the heart of

Americans' abhorrence of the Soviet and Chinese totalitarian Communist systems. On the other hand, many Catholic immigrants who came to the United States for economic survival and opportunity experienced some fear of a society without moral and spiritual authority at its core.

In that context of identities born of experience and deeply held values passed from parent to child, issues such as the following produce continuing tensions between Catholics and Protestants:

- Papal authority vs. a participatory polity remains a key issue both practically and in terms of what it symbolizes.

- The exclusiveness of the Roman Catholic eucharist and the inclusiveness of the Reformed communion service are constant irritants and reminders.

- Views on the role of women are highly emotional and practical issues.

- While views of family planning and abortion cut across denominations, these issues have a special Catholic dimension.

One could hold either of two views about lay dialogue on such subjects: (1) These issues of authority, governance, doctrine can only be resolved at an official level because only officials have the authority to speak for institutions. (2) Officials must address technical issues, but they are not likely to get to underlying human issues. Besides, they seem paralyzed. Lay persons have a need to reassure each other on these issues at a human level. Individuals need to tell each other how they really feel on these issues. For that purpose, dialogue is an appropriate instrument.

Third—problems within the larger society. Lay Christians already work together in dealing with problems in their communities and in their larger bodies politic. Where those issues are divisive, lay persons can use the instrument of dialogue in a Christian setting as a means of enlarging the possibility of reconciliation around those issues.

The Approach: Sustained Dialogue

What follows this introduction is a dialogue process presented in generic style for use in a wide range of situations. Lay Christians will need to internalize the process and adapt it for use according to their particular needs. The sucessful use of this process depends on its prayerful application to each situation and the capacity of moderators to draw on their own inner resources to guide the interaction of participants into creative reconciling work together.

The approach—explained more fully in the paper that follows—is sustained, purposeful dialogue in which participants work together through a series of meetings to design ways to change their relationships. This kind of dialogue differs from a good one-time conversation or a well-prepared study group because its purpose is to produce lasting change in relationships between alienated groups. This kind of dialogue is different from the efforts of mediators and negotiators to achieve formal agreements. The purpose is to build common ground from which to strengthen working relationships.

In this process of dialogue, participants constantly keep alive a two-part agenda. They discuss the concrete problems and issues that they face together or that alienate them, but at the same time they probe the dynamics of the relationships that underlie the problems. They probe the human dimensions of the problems—the relationships that have to be changed if obstacles are to be overcome.

But they do not stop at changing relationships within the dialogue group. They work together to design steps for taking the change they have experienced in their dialogue out into the larger groups from which they come.

This process involves identifying about a dozen individuals who are concerned enough about a situation to be willing to talk about it in depth. Participants must reflect the main interests and groups involved. They must be willing to meet for several hours at a time regularly over months. They must have influence in the groups with which they identify. An experienced moderator or co-moderators will be needed.

Lay individuals and groups in Roman Catholic and Reformed Churches who feel they could contribute to unifying the People of God through the experience of strengthening their own relationships are invited to reflect on the process described here to determine whether it could be useful to them.

Overview of the Dialogue

The approach offered here is *sustained dialogue—an interactive process designed to change relationships over time.* It is a political process in which participants probe the dynamics of even the most destructive relationships and gradually develop a capacity together to design steps to change them.

Dialogue by its very nature provides the context for developing and changing relationships. The key to dialogue is listening carefully to another person's interests and feelings so as to understand where common ground exists for pursuing common interests and why differences remain. It illuminates real fears, misperceptions, and interests and can establish ground for mutual respect. It produces insight into how groups can interact so as to change their relationship.

The following pages describe *a process of dialogue that grows and deepens through five stages:*

1. People *decide to engage in dialogue* because they feel a need to build or change a relationship to resolve a problem that hurts their interests.

2. They come together to talk—to *map the elements of those problems and the relationships responsible* for creating and dealing with them.

3. They *probe specific problems to uncover the dynamics of underlying relationships* and even begin to see ways into those relationships to change them.

4. Together, they *design a scenario of steps* to be taken in a larger arena to change those relationships.

5. Finally, they devise ways to *put that scenario into action.* By the end of the dialogue, participants have moved from wariness of each other to a close working and even personal relationship with insight into how to share their experience more widely.

These five stages are not rigid; one does not fully end before the next begins. Participants move back and forth across the stages. But the framework suggested provides a checklist of the work that needs to be done if the dialogue is to have a sense of purpose and direction and if it is to produce change in conflictual relationships. Depending on time available, a moderator will need to allocate time among stages, but he or she should allow time for the group to get "stuck" in Stages Two and Three.

The stages of the dialogue are detailed in the following pages. Key questions for the moderator appear in italics. They are suggestions for the moderator's guidance. Each moderator will need to understand the purpose behind these generic questions and fashion specific questions appropriate for the particular group and the problems it faces.

[NOTE: An Organizer's and Moderator's Manual for the conduct of sustained dialogue is available from the Charles F. Kettering Foundation, 444 North Capitol Street, NW—Suite 434, Washington, DC 20001-1512.]

Stage One: Deciding to Engage in Dialogue

The *purposes* at this stage—before people ever come together in dialogue—are (1) to find appropriate participants; (2) to reach agreement that they will meet; and (3) to produce understanding on the nature, purpose, and broad ground rules of the dialogue. Four *questions* must be addressed: (1) Who will take the initiative? (2) Who will be the participants? (3) How can resistance to dialogue be overcome? (4) Under what conditions will the dialogue take place?

Who Will Take the Initiative?

A dialogue can be initiated in one of two ways: either concerned individuals from the communities in tension can seek out like-minded people in the other community, or an interested group outside the field of tension can try to bring people together.

Sometimes, a person or a group inside one community takes the initiative, or individuals from each group cautiously reach out to the other. The advantage of this approach is that participants would then take ownership of the dialogue from the beginning. But often this is difficult, and a catalyst from outside is needed.

A so-called third party normally begins by talking in depth with many individuals directly involved to gather knowledge about the interests, feelings, and positions of each group. The purpose is to identify individuals who might participate in the dialogue and to define tentatively key problems and how they will be discussed.

The identity of the convener or convener team will make a difference. If from within the communities, co-conveners could include a person from each community who is respected by the other side(s). Alternatively, one person from within or outside, trusted by all involved, could serve this function. If there is a third-party initiative, a team with broad experience across communities will bring to the discussions different perspectives and impart a neutral character.

Who Will Be the Participants?
At the beginning, the participants are normally individuals who are well respected in their communities. Later, they will seek ways to draw a larger number of people in their communities into dialogue or action. They are individuals free to listen and to share—not compelled to defend or posture.

Usually, participants are individuals who have concluded that the present situation hurts their interests to an extent that is becoming intolerable. As individuals, they are ready to risk working toward change, but they need to enlarge the credibility of their perspective in the community. (Learning what brings people to this conclusion in a situation is critical.)

One might start by talking with two or three dozen people, but for the initial dialogue, select approximately ten people who represent main perspectives in the communities, noting that there are divisions within groups as well as between them. It may not be possible to enlist a fully representative group at first, but it may be better to begin than to seek perfection. Eventually, the aim is to spread the dialogue experience in the community to lay foundations for changing relationships.

How Can Resistance to Dialogue Be Overcome?

Often, potential participants are reluctant to commit themselves to in-depth dialogue. Sometimes, they deny a problem exists at all because they are not ready to deal with it. Others blame the other group for being unwilling to talk. The challenge is to cause people to see a long-term problem as warranting a systematic dialogue.

People often deny there is a problem. "But we do talk," they say.

Would you be content to leave this relationship to your children this way? Or do you see feelings under the surface that are unhealthy? Should an effort be made now to try to deal with them? How do others feel?

Why don't people want to talk? What are they reluctant about?

Another challenge, even when people are talking, is to generate realization that they are not really talking about the problems in relationships that actually cause problems. Groups may have learned in their own self-interest to work together in common projects or workplaces, but they carefully avoid talking about underlying tensions in their relationships in order not to disrupt minimal necessary cooperation.

If you think seriously about present relationships, could you tell some stories about underlying tensions? Or do you really feel that no tensions exist?

Can you give examples of what kind of talking goes on now? Does it go to the heart of the underlying relationships that cause tensions? Or does it skirt around them?

When tensions have risen or already erupted in some way, persons on both sides may believe that time is on their side or that it will reduce tensions. The problem is how to convince people that tensions usually deepen rather than disappear if not dealt with.

What are the costs of continuing alienation and suspicion to you and your community?

Does anyone gain from this alienation? If so, who and how?

What will your children face if relationships continue as they are?

How much longer can you tolerate this situation? When is enough enough? Is this the kind of relationship you want your children to grow up in?

Under What Conditions Will the Dialogue Take Place?

It is important to explain that the dialogue will take place in a space owned by all and safe for all. Often, meeting in a neutral site will help participants feel safe. To give the dialogue purpose and direction, the primary condition to which the parties must agree is that the purpose is to probe for underlying elements of tense or conflictual relationships between them that must be changed to improve conditions or to resolve conflict. Certain ground rules should be agreed:

- Participants represent only themselves. They reflect views in their communities, but they do not formally represent organizations or groups.

- Participants will interact civilly, listen actively to each other, and allow each to present views fully.

- It is necessary to discuss both concrete issues and the feelings behind them. Feelings are expressed with mutual respect.

- Participants observe time limits on statements to allow genuine dialogue.

- Nothing said in the dialogue is repeated outside that room.

The Transition and Product of Stage One

Precipitating a decision to meet may require a traumatic event, a conciliatory gesture by one of the groups, or a third-party invitation. Whatever the situation, someone needs to propose, "Shall we meet and try to talk about our relationship?"

The *product* at the end of Stage One is an agreement among prospective participants to engage in a dialogue over some period for particular purposes. The understanding will set time, place, convening authority, financial responsibility if necessary, and ground rules.

Stage Two: Mapping the Relationship Together

The *purposes* when participants first come together are (1) to get out on the table the main problems that affect the relationships among them and (2) to be sure the group identifies all of the significant relationships that are responsible for creating these problems and that would need to be changed to resolve them. We speak of "mapping"—or drawing a mental picture—of the whole complex of relationships involved in the important problems participants face.

When a group first comes together, it is important to reiterate, consolidate, and affirm the agreement that was reached in the previous stage. The purpose, agenda, and ground rules should be reaffirmed by the whole group together. It is particularly important—because it is not the usual way of talking about issues—to restate the dual agenda.

> *We will always have two subjects on the agenda at the same time. One will be the specific problems we need to talk about. But at the same time, we want to talk directly about the relationships underneath those problems. Trying to talk straightforwardly about our relationships is what makes this meeting different from others.*

Mapping the Problems and the Relationships Underlying Them

It may be desirable as a group sits down to spend some time in which participants would begin getting to know each other in the context of the problems on the agenda:

> *In introducing yourselves, could each of you please share with the group some experience you have had with the relationships we are going to discuss?*

After substantive introductions, the dialogue might begin with three questions:

What are the main problems you face and would like to resolve?

How do these problems affect the interests of the group with which you identify?

What are the important relationships responsible for creating these problems that would need to be changed in order to resolve them?

The questions should vary to address the specific problems the group faces. But their aim is to identify and to define both the critical problems and the relationships underlying them. That dual agenda cannot be repeated too often because it is not a familiar one to most participants.

As each problem is discussed, it is also essential to probe real interests— not just the objectively defined interests but also the underlying explanations of why something is important to a person or group. A moderator should ask some variation of the following question often enough to make the point that this dialogue is different from the usual academic or policy discussion:

*Why do you **really** care? Why is that so important to your group?*

Through most of this discussion, as participants lay out what is on their minds, the moderator will play a relatively permissive role—except for encouraging participants to respect the right and time of each to speak. But on two points—identifying underlying relationships and probing deeply into interests—the moderator will need to press harder.

A thought for the moderator. As participants discuss problems, they will often mention conditions they would like to see evolve that would better serve the interests of all. Developing a picture of preferred alternative relationships is work that will be done more systematically at the end of the next stage. But it can help lighten the atmosphere in the group to encourage hope. Without losing the main focus of this stage, it may be useful to focus such comments for later use with questions such as the following:

What kind of relationships would better serve your interests?

What would you have to change to create those relationships?

What would you want or need to preserve from the present situation? Why?

Who else would have to be involved if you were to make those changes?

Again briefly, without losing the main purpose of identifying problems and the relationships that cause them, the moderator may find it helpful to use comments for a moment that identify for later use the obstacles that stand in the way of moving in the direction that interests dictate.

Given the kind of relationships you would like to create, what are the main obstacles standing in the way of moving in that direction? We'll note them for later use.

Given the direction in which you would like relationships to move and the barriers in the way, how would you define the main obstacles you face?

Hope is part of a present situation. These questions are not intended to throw the group into focusing on solutions. They simply start the group thinking about the costs of the present situation. Obstacles are also part of the present situation; identifying them helps define key problems.

Transition: Focusing the Agenda and Overcoming Resistance
When a relatively full picture of the problems and the relationships behind them has emerged, the moderator will begin shifting gears to bring this stage to a close. The task is to cluster problems and to select two to four for the group to talk about in greater depth. One way to start this *transition* to the next stage is to ask questions such as these:

Given the problems you have identified, what are the problems you most need to work on in greater depth?

Given the realities of the situation, which problem should you work on first? What can you learn from the order in which you have placed the problems?

The aim is to produce an agreed list of the problems the group considers most important. In this stage, the purpose has been to map the field—to identify a broad range of problems and the relationships that would have to be changed to deal with those problems. This has been a survey; that is why it is called "mapping." In contrast, in the next stage the group will take *one problem at a time* and probe it deeply and systematically. Often, the group will agree that one problem must be dealt with before others can be considered seriously. There will be more time in the next meeting(s) to discuss the substance of each problem and more time to probe deeply into the dynamics of the relationships responsible for creating that problem.

In the next stage, the moderator will play a more active role in keeping the dialogue to the point and in helping the group to address the difficult probing questions.

Overcoming resistance. Much more difficult sometimes than reaching agreement on a list of specific problems for focusing the next stage of the dialogue is overcoming remaining resistance to a sustained dialogue. Resistance is likely when dialogue focuses on problems that participants know will involve their reaching out to others in ways that acknowledge the legitimacy of some of the other participants' views or make themselves vulnerable. It is one thing to agree on subjects to be discussed but quite another to be ready to talk about those subjects in a way that shows understanding of the other's feelings and way of thinking—or reveals one's own. Overcoming that resistance is critical to the transition to Stage Three. Two possible approaches:

Option 1—A "walk through history." One approach is to stop and deal with the resistance head-on—to have participants listen respectfully as each pours out her or his experiences, grievances, and hurts. Each participant tells her or his own story.

Tell us how the problem began for you or your group. Who was responsible? Can you tell us how your group thinks the other group would tell this story?

The purpose is to begin a change in perceptions and stereotypes: "I didn't know that's how it looked to you. . . . We should forgive each other and try to start our relationship again." This approach tackles resistance at its heart and can open the door to changed relationships, but it requires a block of time and risks bogging down in recriminations and might even trigger an outburst of emotion that could destroy the dialogue. If carried through with mutual respect and human concern, it can produce a transforming experience and lay a foundation for reconciliation.

Option 2—Address obstacles through concrete problems. Some groups may not be ready for such an intense experience at this early moment in their relationship. In such cases, some variant of the "walk through history" may be reserved for later. Meanwhile, an alternative is to march ahead with discussion of the practical problems identified but actively seek out and use the moments when feeling is expressed and might be dealt with constructively to probe a particular obstacle to dialogue.

The Products of Stage Two
First is the moderator's judgment that resistance has been sufficiently overcome and that the quality of the dialogue has begun to change—that the participants can talk with each other instead of just stating views and that they show readiness to settle down to serious discussion of specific problems, one at a time.

Second is a clear definition and understanding of two to four concrete problems to be discussed in depth, one at a time. This should be an agreed list. These are problems that—if discussed in detail—will reveal the dynamics of the relationships that must be changed if the problems are to be dealt with.

Homework Assignment
It often proves useful to provide participants with a way of channeling their reflections as they evolve between meetings. At this stage, the moderator might simply ask participants:

> We have identified several specific problems to discuss more deeply at our next meeting. Could you come next time with a carefully worded statement of the problem(s) as you would describe it (them)?

Stage Three: Probing the Dynamics of Relationships to Generate a Will to Change

The *purpose* in this stage is to use in-depth probing of specific problems to *generate the will* within the participants to change the conflictual relationships so as to deal with the problems that face them. Only when participants feel a compelling need for change and accept personal responsibility for trying to make change happen can the dialogue move beyond this stage. To achieve that aim, the *tasks* are

1. to *shift the mode of discourse* from explanation of each side's position to genuine dialogue, where participants talk with each other, respond to each other, and ask each other clarifying questions;

2. to *probe the problems* that participants have agreed they most need to work on and to use that analysis as a vehicle to *illuminate the dynamics of the relationships* that are responsible for creating the problem and that must be changed if it is to be dealt with; and eventually

3. by asking the participants to assess where present relationships are leading, to create conditions in which participants *generate the will to change* the situation and muster the determination to design ways of changing the destructive relationships that stand in the way of change.

The moderator will need to play a more directive role. For example, strong feelings may flare up. The moderator should control some, and choose others to probe the dynamics of the interactions involved. The moderator will also need to discipline the dialogue to keep it focused on the dual agenda—one problem at a time and to probe the relationships that create the problem and could change it.

Working with the Agenda to Probe Relationships

Confirming the agenda. An agenda—a list of problems—was agreed in general terms at the end of the last session. Since some time will probably have passed, it is a good idea to confirm, revise, or develop that agenda more precisely and to confirm the approach of sticking to one problem at a time and using each subject to probe the relationships behind it.

Would someone restate the problems the group agreed to work on? Why are they important? Do changes need to be made? Are you agreed?

Can we list the subjects to be discussed in some logical order?

Do we agree to stick with each subject long enough to reach an understanding?

Do we all understand the two related subjects on our agenda? We will be talking about specific problems, but we also want to probe the relationships behind them.

Probing problems and relationships. Once an agenda of two to four problems is agreed upon, the dialogue turns to each problem, one at a time. Dialogue begins with *the problem.*

How would each of you define the elements of this problem?

How does this problem affect your group's interests—what you really care about?

Is there enough harm to your interests to cause a desire for change? If so, what needs must be met? If not, how can the situation be managed to minimize harm?

What directions might constructive change take? What are the options? What are the advantages and disadvantages for each group?

How have you or your group contributed to creating this problem? What changes could you or your group initiate uni-laterally in order to bring about some change?

Where could you find common ground in moving toward a new situation?

To this point, the talk may be similar to a thoughtful public deliberation about a serious subject that affects a community—with one significant difference: the participants come from communities that feel some suspicion toward each other. More than in most situations, no problem will be constructively dealt with unless the uneasy relationships behind it are changed. In *probing relationships* that underlie the problems, there will not be time or patience for a complete analysis, but the moderator can use questions such as these to help participants probe:

What are the main groups involved in the problem we are discussing?

How are individuals in your group personally affected?

From your group's perspective, can you describe how other groups see themselves? What experience and heritage have produced their self-images?

Could you describe the other groups' interests, in your own words? Can you see why those interests are important to them?

How do these groups normally interact? Do they fight, bargain, posture, talk? Can you explain why?

What groups seem powerful to you? What is power in this situation? If power is the capacity to influence events, who is really powerful? Why?

Do you sense any way in which parties to some of these relationships observe certain limits in dealing with each other?

How does each group perceive the other? Why do you think that is the case? In what ways does your group hold others responsible for your situation? Do you see ways of changing those perceptions?

Do these groups have any significant common interests? What are they?

Assessing Relationships and Their Direction: Generating the Will to Change

Generating the will to change is the ultimate goal in Stage Three. One way to move toward a judgment that change is necessary and worth the cost is to lead participants to the judgments that what should be done cannot be done as long as the present state of relationships persists and that the costs of not changing are greater. This can be done by bringing the group to a pause for an assessment of where present relationships are taking the situation.

Where is the situation going? At some point—perhaps after a break—the moderator shifts gears to ask the group to imagine how the present situation might unfold. The participants could visualize a number of paths along which the situation might develop if nothing is done in the interim to reverse current trends. This usually involves an assessment of the costs to each party in each case. The moderator does not require the participants to agree on the likelihood of any of these developments. It is essential that each hear the other's perspectives about how the current situation might unfold.

> Given the present interactions between groups, where is the situation going? Do you like what you foresee?

> How would each line of development affect each group's interests?

> How would each line of development affect the capacities of each group to deal effectively with this problem—or to work with other groups where outcomes depend on collaboration?

> Can you live with what you see developing? Can your children live with it? Or do you see a serious need for change? What would you be willing to do to promote a desire for change among all who are affected?

Is change possible? What would it require? This dialogue should have led to thought about the consequences of continuing the present situation. If a will to change seems to be emerging, the next questions will be:

Are others interested in change? Why? Is there some common ground?

What changes in relationships would be needed to move to the kind of community/country that would deal effectively with this problem and would better serve your interests?

What changes in the mix of elements in these relationships would be needed?

What does each group do to perpetuate this situation?

What can you change in your own group's actions?

The Transition and Products of Stage Three
Is the group thinking together? Is there a will to change?

The *first* task in bringing Stage Three to closure and moving to the next level of dialogue is to consolidate the group's experience in genuine dialogue so as to get participants thinking together in an operational way. Is the group really talking and thinking together about problems?

Second, it will be necessary to determine whether the group seems to have the will to take that next step and to begin talking together about how to design change. If so:

Since you seem to feel that some change in the way your groups relate to each other would serve the interests of most groups, would you be willing to think together about steps each group could take alongside changes by other groups to make change possible?

If you would consider such a task, we would begin our next session with a working agenda to help you design a series of interactive steps.

If not, why is it still difficult for your group to change or to work with others?

The *products* of this stage are (1) the experience of an increasingly direct and probing dialogue that deepens and begins to change relationships within the group; (2) a new body of insight into the perceptions, feelings, and conceptual frameworks of others; (3) an outline of how present relationships between the parties need to change in order to produce conditions that might lead to a more desirable way of dealing with problems; and (4) above all these, a judgment that the costs of continuing the present situation and relationships outweigh the costs of trying to change them. The critical product—and Stage Three cannot end without it—is the *generation of a will to change*.

Homework Assignment

If the group has enough time to devote one session to the obstacles to change and another to steps for overcoming those obstacles, the questions below could be separated—one each night. If not, they will need to be posed together.

> *Before the next meeting, would you please write two lists:*
> * *List obstacles to moving in the direction you want to move.*
> * *List possible steps for overcoming those obstacles.*

Stage Four: Experiencing Relationships— Building Scenarios

The *purpose* in this stage is to bring members of the group into a new way of thinking together about how to generate the change they would like to see happen. Figuratively, they are no longer sitting across the table talking to each other; they are sitting side-by-side to design ways to change relationships they all agree need to be changed to deal with problems in the interests of each. In a sense, the group becomes a microcosm of the larger relationships involved.

The Vehicle for Change: Scenario-Building

The vehicle for change is posing a task that requires participants to design steps to change relationships between their groups. By thinking together about how to change a situation and the relationships that cause it, they themselves experience what the relationship would have to become in the larger society if the desired changes were to be accomplished. They also experience the internal obstacles to change and agonize over how individuals will overcome those obstacles.

We call this *task* "scenario-building" because participants are asked to list obstacles to change, to think of steps to overcome those obstacles, and to identify actors who can take those steps. Then they are asked to arrange these steps so that they interact—one responding to another— so they work to reinforce each other to build momentum and gradually to create a new atmosphere. This interactive sequence of steps is like an unfolding scene in a drama. If the group is small, it may stay together for this exercise, but it may be desirable to divide even a small group into still smaller groups in order to foster the experience of thinking together and engaging in deeper discussion of obstacles to change.

Establishing the *starting point* can stem from previous dialogue.

> At the end of the last session, we asked: "What changes in relationships are needed to deal with the problems we have discussed?" Would someone review the responses? Do they need to be refined?

With a starting point established, participants are then asked to perform four tasks:

First, they are to *identify obstacles* to moving in the direction they have determined that they want to pursue. They will certainly identify tangible obstacles such as the positions of opposing parties, the lack of resources, the opposing objectives of different groups, the inflamed emotions in a heated conflict.

But they will also need to probe beneath those to be sure they have brought to the surface the underlying human dimension of those obstacles—the fears, the historic grievances, the misperceptions, the stereotypes, the wounds from the past, the human interests. Often these are greater obstacles to change than objective components of a situation for which there may well be technical solutions.

*What are the main obstacles to changing relationships in the
ways needed?*

*Are those the real obstacles or are there also other deeper rooted
obstacles?*

*Are you addressing the fears, misperceptions, grievances,
animosities?*

Second, once the group has developed a full list of obstacles, it needs to
develop a parallel *list of steps that could help overcome those obstacles.*
Some of these may be official steps. Others may be steps taken by
nongovernmental organizations. All of them are steps designed for the
purpose of removing the obstacles identified. These steps will include
concrete measures to change conditions that one group finds unjust or
harmful. The steps also need to include ways of dealing with misperceptions and underlying human fears and hurts. That area is not as often
thought of in normal political life. It includes public statements or acts
that symbolize contrition and forgiveness—recognition of harm that has
been done and apology for it.

*Name as many steps as you can think of to remove each of the
obstacles you have listed. Since no single action may be enough
to change longstanding relationships, a series of steps will be
needed for cumulative impact.*

*You need to pay special attention to the human obstacles. They
are often the most serious obstacles, but we are least familiar in
dealing with them. You also need to pay attention to the
obstacles your group poses or are responsible for.*

Third, once the participants have developed a significant list of obstacles
and steps to overcome them, they need to *identify who can take those
steps.* Often, the first attempt at a list of actors reveals that participants
are naming steps for others to take—none that they themselves will take
responsibility for initiating. The exercise has little real meaning until
participants themselves are personally engaged. They will not experience
the cost of changing critical relationships until they struggle with those
costs inside themselves.

Who can take the steps you have listed?

What steps could you persuade your own group to take?

What steps would you personally take responsibility for?

Fourth, these steps need to be arranged in some realistic *interactive sequence*. In order to have the impact of changing a relationship, these steps must be placed in a pattern of action, response, and further response. If the purpose is to change the dynamics of the interaction among groups, then the steps must be taken interactively. For instance, Party A may be able to take step one only if it is assured that Party B will respond; Party B may agree, but only if Party A will respond with step three. We have often called this sequence of interactive steps a "scenario" because it resembles the way a playwright builds an act in a play with the interactions among the characters on the stage building a situation and then moving it forward.

> *What steps could your group take first? What is the exact objective?*
>
> *What responses from other groups are required to make your steps possible? Must those responses be agreed upon before the first steps can be taken? Why?*
>
> *Is it possible to cluster steps to enhance impact? What impact do you want?*
>
> *When several significant steps have been taken, is there a way to create public recognition that something different is beginning to happen?*
>
> *Is a cluster of steps possible to dramatize and consolidate the new trend?*

The Products and Transition of Stage Four

It is difficult to say which is the more important *product* of this thinking together—the scenario itself as a plan for future action or the relationships within the group that have been changed by creating the scenario. The scenario does provide a plan that could be taken out of the group into organizations where participants are influential or into governments as suggestions for a new course of action. But the experience with key relationships within the participants themselves may lead them to insights into change that are even more important.

This stage ends when participants are satisfied with the scenario, but the delicate question hanging over the group will be: "What do we do with this plan?" They have a choice: they can simply treat their experience as a learning exercise within the group—perhaps to be shared with a few close colleagues outside the group. Or the group could say. "This is too important to leave where it is. We have to find a way to put this into action."

The choice of whether or not to go on to act together to put these insights into play in the political arena may be difficult for many. So there may be at the end of this stage a deep discussion of the dangers and advantages of taking the next step. The participants may have very difficult personal and group choices to make. A moderator will not try to influence this deliberation. Participants may need time before a next meeting to decide. Determining what to do is the work of Stage Five.

Stage Five: Acting Together
One of the greatest challenges in this process is how to take the transforming insights and experiences generated within the dialogue out into the body politic. How can a small group translate personal experiences of reconciliation into societal change? One must be realistic about expectations. At the same time, one must ask: "How far can this process reach?"

Within the progress of this dialogue, the *purpose* at this stage is to develop practical ways the scenario(s) developed in Stage Four might be put into action. Whether and how participants will take action is still a matter of difficult choice for each of them.

But in the larger context of the whole dialogue, individual participants will already have taken their insights, between meetings, back into their communities and councils. During this dialogue—if it has continued over time—participants may have taken new, more influential positions, founded new organizations, or formed new networks. It is actually worth asking as soon as a group moves into Stage Four: "What can each of you do to develop dialogues like this in your own communities or groups?"

The immediate *task* at this stage is for the participants to reflect together on what is possible for them. The moderator should revert to a more permissive style. Her or his role is to help the participants define and explore the different options, and to help them think through the pros and cons of each option. The moderator could draw upon other experiences to outline some choices for the group to discuss. One difficulty is to help participants deal with their own doubt that a small group of citizens could have significant impact on the course of events.

One way to begin—and to put doubts into perspective—is to ask the group to *consider their own capacities to marshal resources for change.* Often, as individuals think about the associations and networks of which they are a part, they begin to see what results old and new relationships might produce. They may begin to visualize what citizens outside government can accomplish simply by committing themselves to work together. That will be even more true if some are already in influential positions.

> *What can you personally or organizations and groups you relate to do to carry out parts of the scenario(s) you have developed?*

Course One. The participants focus on what personal use they can make of the ideas generated in the group. They might share those insights with governments and/or with their individual organizations, but without any effort on their part to get the recommendations implemented. The advantage of Course One is that it is feasible and can happen in a variety of ways with minimal cost. The disadvantage is that such an approach may not have a direct impact on government policy. Governments usually ignore citizens outside of government.

Course Two. The group becomes an action group. It would assume responsibility for lobbying the authorities to make sure that its recommendations are implemented. In the extreme case, the group would assume responsibility for implementing those recommendations itself. The advantage is that the group would benefit tremendously from working together on implementation. The disadvantage of Course Two is that the group could become absorbed in a course of action and could lose its capacity to step back and reflect on its actions, although this might be overcome by building into the group's work a sequence of acting and then stepping back to reflect on the actions taken and their consequences.

Course Three. Enlarge the meeting space and invite periodically to the meeting participants from the government and/or other conflicting groups. An advantage of Course Three is to make it possible to create a subset of the group to discuss a particular problem while preserving the integrity of the original group itself. A disadvantage is that it may not produce change or action in the short term.

Course Four. The group from very early in its dialogue might keep in mind the possible strategy of proliferating dialogue groups. The purpose would be gradually to create a critical mass of people who recognize the need for changing relationships and who are committed to actions for doing so.

A variation of this approach is at least to ask at each stage of the dialogue who else needs to be at the table or who else needs to be kept abreast of the progress of the dialogue and to discuss strategies for involving them. Often, if there are no overt hostilities, people deny that there is any problem.

The Products of Stage Five
One *product* is that the participants of the group will experience working together on implementation strategies over a period of time. As they do, they will gain deeper and deeper insight into the obstacles and opportunities each group experiences.

An even more significant *product*—if the group commits itself to seeing that its scenario is carried out—is the potential for spreading its way of thinking and its scenario of actions more and more widely. Tangible impact is possible.

A SHORT HISTORY OF THE PRESBYTERIAN/REFORMED— ROMAN CATHOLIC CONSULTATION

by Dr. Eugene J. Fisher

The Christian people are one in their faith in Jesus Christ. The majority of the People of God—spoken of routinely as "The Laity"—celebrate their call to service in the Church and in the world in churches that remain divided. As St. Paul admonished the church at Corinth:

> Now I appeal to you, brothers and sisters, by the name of our Lord Jesus Christ, that all of you be in agreement and that there be no divisions among you, but that you be united in the same mind and the same purpose (1 Cor 1:10).

While Christ calls Christians to be one in him, the ecumenical pilgrimage toward unity is only just beginning. By baptism and by faith in the triune God, Christians are already in real—if yet imperfect—unity. Discussion of the mission and calling of the laity within the Church, and as Church in the world, should be a contribution toward deepening Christian unity and challenging the leadership and structures of our churches to promote the full unity to which Christians are called in Christ. The 1991 Canberra meeting of the World Council of Churches articulated this biblical vision as a call to full communion:

> The purpose of God according to Holy Scripture is to gather the whole of creation under the Lordship of Christ Jesus in whom, by the power of the Holy Spirit, all are brought into communion with God. The Church is the foretaste of this communion with God and with one another. The grace of our Lord Jesus Christ, the love of God and the communion of the Holy Spirit enable the one Church to live as sign of the reign of God and servant of the reconciliation with God, promised and provided for the whole creation. The purpose of the Church is to unite people with

Christ in the power of the Spirit, to manifest communion in prayer and action and thus to point to the fullness of communion with God, humanity and the whole creation in the glory of the kingdom.

The unity of the Church to which we are called is a *koinonia* given and expressed in the common confession of apostolic faith; a common sacramental life entered by one baptism and celebrated together in one eucharistic fellowship; a common life in which members and ministries are mutually recognized and reconciled; and a common mission witnessing to all people to the gospel of God's grace and serving the whole of creation. The goal of the search for full communion is realized when all the churches are able to recognize in one another the one, holy, catholic and apostolic church in its fullness. This full communion will be expressed on the local and universal levels through conciliar forms of life and action. In such communion churches are bound in all aspects of their life together at all levels in confessing the one faith and engaging in worship and witness, deliberation and action (The World Council of Churches' Canberra Statement on *The Unity of the Church as Koinonia*, cited in Michael Kinnamon, ed., *Signs of the Spirit*, Geneva, WCC, and Grand Rapids, Wm. B.).

It is within this vision of the Church as a conciliar communion that the dialogues of the Reformed Churches, with the Lutherans and in the Consultation on Church Union, take place. Likewise, the Roman Catholic Church in its quest for full communion with the Orthodox, Anglican, Lutheran, and other Churches has based its discussions on a similar biblical foundation. This vision of a reconciled Church enables Christians to witness in the home, neighborhood, work, nation, and world. It is our hope that this volume will contribute to this building of full communion.

The Reformed Churches since the time of John Calvin have preserved the Church's strong commitment to collegiality and participation of the laity in governance and decision making. The *Catechism of the Catholic Church* (United States Catholic Conference, 1994) renews this tradition from the common heritage:

. . . the faithful, who by Baptism are incorporated into Christ and integrated into the people of God, are made sharers in their particular way in the priestly, prophetic, and kingly office of Christ, and have their own part to play in the mission of the whole Christian people in the Church and in the world (CCC, no. 897).

This "special vocation"—the common heritage of both communities—is lived out both within the worship life and governance of the Christian community, and in the world "according to the grace and charisms which the Lord has been pleased to bestow on them" (CCC, no. 910).

Since the mid-1960s, the Christian Churches, Reformed and Roman Catholic among them, have been in dialogue, seeking full unity in faith, sacramental life, mission, and decision making. Through the World and National Council of Churches, proposals have been made to promote this unity. The specific elements of a conciliar communion are the context of these dialogues, as noted above. Agreements have been proposed for Reformed and Roman Catholic reconciliation on a worldwide level in two series of dialogues: "The Presence of Christ in Church and World" (1977) and "Towards a Common Understanding of the Church" (1984). Conversations between our churches in the United States take account of these worldwide contributions toward our unity as churches.

This statement on laity is a result of Round V of the Roman Catholic—Presbyterian/Reformed Consultation jointly sponsored by the Bishops' Committee for Ecumenical and Interreligious Affairs of the National Conference of Catholic Bishops and the Caribbean and North American Area Council of the World Alliance of Reformed Churches (Presbyterian and Congregational).[1] The latter include major Calvinist Churches with German, Scottish, Puritan, and Dutch heritage in the United States.

Two of the WARC members represent reunited Christian Churches. The United Church of Christ in 1957 brought together churches with Lutheran, Calvinist, and Campbellite traditions. In 1983, the United Presbyterian USA and Presbyterian Church U.S. merged to heal the breach in the Presbyterian Church brought about by the Civil War more than 100 years earlier. Cumberland Presbyterian, Hungarian Reformed, and Reformed Church in America have also participated in these dialogues.

The American dialogue between our two confessional traditions, which has been going on since 1965, thus brings to the table not only theoretical but also practical expertise in ecumenism. Previous discussions have innovated several areas of ecumenical reflection.

The first Round of discussions commenced in July 1965, co-chaired by Mr. Richard L. Davies of Washington and Bishop Ernest Unterkoefler of Charleston, South Carolina. Bishop Unterkoefler held the Catholic chair through Round IV, until his death in 1992. Mr. Davies was succeeded in 1967 by Dr. Robert Moss of Lancaster, Pennsylvania, for the duration of the first Round. Dr. Andrew Harsanyi of the Hungarian Reformed Church in American served as cochair from 1972 to 1992. He participated as well in the planning meeting that established the topic for the present Round V.

The first Round took up topics still of central interest for the ecumenical endeavor. It discussed "the Holy Spirit in the Reform and Renewal of the Church"; "Revelation, Scripture and Tradition"; "The Development of Doctrine"; and "Ministry and Order of the Church." While there was no joint statement from this first Round, the papers and summary of discussion were published in a volume entitled *Reconsiderations*.[2] Commenting jointly on the discussions at the end of the volume, Daniel J. O'Hanlon, SJ, and Robert McAfee Brown noted that the "flexibility of the first two centuries" in the "forms of ministry of the Church," while "providing no warrant for naively turning back the clock seventeen centuries, did at least suggest that the present pattern was not an absolute."[3] Without taking away from subsequent consultations, it may be said that the present Round on laity takes up a quarter of a century later the challenge of the first Round from a different yet compatible vantage point. Thus does the search for Christian unity cycle back time and again to its core themes and urging of the Spirit.

The first truly joint statement of the consultation was devoted to the topic "The Ministry of the Church."[4] The parallel statement of the consultation's other section, on Worship and Mission, entitled "Women in the Church" has been reprinted in the volume *Ecumenical Documents IV: Building Unity*.[5]

The second Round of the consultation produced a very substantive statement that sought to project the nature of *The Unity We Seek*[6] in belief, structure, and worship. The action recommendations at the end of each reflection on "what is essential" remain challenging both nationally and in local congregations.

The third and fourth Rounds discussed the relationship between ethical issues and ecumenism. To what extent, it was asked, are differing stances on personal and social ethical questions Church-dividing? In *Ethics and the Search for Christian Unity*[7] in 1980, the consultation took up two topics of great sensitivity and difficulty for our religious communities. The joint "Statement on Abortion" from *Ethics and the Search for Christian Unity* still serves as a model for what can be said together by two believing communities despite real differences in theory and practice. Likewise, the "Statement on Human Rights," which focussed especially on the case of South Africa, while illustrating a closer common moral vision on one level, also surfaced some real differences in how one ameliorates a situation both communions view as inherently immoral. The end of apartheid in South Africa has shown the importance of the Churches' human rights witness.

The statement of the fourth Round in 1988, *Partners in Peace and Education*,[8] centered on two topics "Church and Nuclear Warfare" and "Church and School." The consultation first discussed together the 1983 Roman Catholic bishops' peace pastoral and several Presbyterian/Reformed statements dealing with the same issue. The conclusions of the joint study revealed remarkable similarity of theological and social-ethical vision and grounding in a shared understanding of human nature. The consultation then grappled with different stances on aid to private education. This section of the statement reflected on very real compatibilities of understanding of the nature and function of the educational process in society and in Church.

There have been numerous contributions to the long pilgrimage toward the unity of the Church. The present contribution on ministry of the laity is grounded in the biblical recognition of the variety and complementarity of God's gifts to all baptized:

> Now there are varieties of gifts, but the same Spirit; and there are varieties of service, but the same Lord; and there are varieties of

activities, but it is the same God who activates all of them in everyone. To each is given the manifestation of the Spirit for the common good. . . . For just as the body is one and has many members, and all the members of the body, though many, are one body, so it is with Christ (1 Cor 12:4-7, 12).

In fact, the Churches have begun to experience wide agreement, not only around the ministry of the whole People of God, but also on the ordained ministry that serves it.

> Though the churches are agreed on their general understanding of the People of God, they differ in their understanding of how the life of the Church is to be ordered. In particular, there are differences concerning the place and forms of the ordained ministry. As they engage it the effort to overcome these differences, the churches need to work from the perspective of the calling of the whole People of God. A common answer needs to be found to the following question: How, according to the will of God and under the guidance of the Holy Spirit, is the life of the Church to be understood and ordered, so that the Gospel may be spread and the community built up in life? (*Baptism, Eucharist and Ministry*, M no. 6; Geneva; World Council of Churches Publisher, 1982).

This study is designed to serve this engagement. In the reconciling ministry of ecumenism, the Christian community recognizes a variety of dynamic and complementary tasks on the pilgrimage toward full communion. Some of these are (1) the dialogue of life, in which the whole People of God interact in faith, witness in the social order, and deepen their spiritual hunger for the full communion to which Christians are called; (2) the technical theological task of reconciling historical differences in the faith of the Church and its ordering, considering the ethical and religious issues that have emerged since the sixteenth century, and applying the best of modern biblical, historical, and contextual scholarship to healing the wounds in the Church's communion; and (3) the ecclesiastical task of bringing these spiritual and theological contributions to reconciliation to bear on the institutional, constitutional, and canonical realities of divided Churches that they may come closer to one another in Christ. The process of reconciliation is a gradual one, moving in such a way that none of the gifts of the Spirit with which diverse church traditions have been endowed in their separation is lost, as the Churches move toward that unity in diversity that is the will of Christ.

Both of our church families are involved in a wide range of dialogues with other Churches, through the Consultation on Church Union, through Faith and Order in World and National Councils, and through bilateral conversations with other partners. It is hoped that, this volume will contribute to these discussions and support the unity of the Churches wherever it is developing. It is also hoped that those who discuss this volume will be enriched by dialogues going on with partners other than the Presbyterian/Reformed and Roman Catholic Churches.

Notes

1   Hereinafter referred to as WARC.

2   Richard L. Davies, Robert V. Moses and Ernest L. Unterkoefler, eds., *Reconsiderations: Roman Catholic/Presbyterian and Reformed Theological Conversations* (New York: World Horizons, 1967).

3   *Reconsiderations*, p. 157.

4   See *The Journal of Ecumenical Studies* 5 (1968): 462–465; 7 (1970): 686–90; and 7 (1972): 589–612.

5   Joseph Burgess and Jeffrey Gros, FSC, eds., *Ecumenical Documents IV: Building Unity* (Mahwah, N.J.: Paulist Press, 1989), 375–383. This volume includes as well all subsequent joint statements to the present, although it does not include background papers. A report on the early meetings, aptly entitled "Explosive Ecumenics," can be found in *The Journal of Ecumenical Studies* 8 (1971): 740ff.

6   Ernest Unterkoefler and Andrew Harsanyi, eds., *The Unity We Seek: A Statement by the Roman Catholic—Presbyterian/Reformed Consultation* (New York: Paulist Press, 1977). Along with background papers, *The Unity We Seek* includes a meeting-by-meeting "history" of the dialogue from 1965 to 1975 written by Eugene M. Burke, CSP.

7   Ernest L. Unterkoefler and Andrew Harsanyi, eds., *Ethics and the Search for Christian Unity* (Washington, D.C: United States Catholic Conference, 1981).

8   Ronald C. White, Jr, and Eugene J. Fisher, eds., *Partners in Peace and Education: Roman Catholic—Presbyterian/Reformed Consultation IV* (Grand Rapids, Mich: William B. Eerdmans Publishing Company, 1988). Includes the text of the joint statement, background papers, and a discussion guide for congregational and educational use.

BIBLIOGRAPHY

by Dr. Eugene J. Fisher
Dr. Dolores R. Leckey

Pertinent Previous Statements of the Roman Catholic— Presbyterian/Reformed Consultation

Committee for Ecumenical and Interreligious Affairs, National Conference of Catholic Bishops, and the North American Area of the World Alliance of Reformed Churches. *Reconsiderations: Roman Catholic/Presbyterian and Reformed Theological Conversations 1966–1967.* New York: World Horizons, Inc., 1967.

Unterkoefler, Ernest L. and Andrew Harsanyi, eds. *The Unity We Seek: A Statement of the Roman Catholic—Presbyterian/Reformed Consultation.* New York: Paulist Press, 1977.

Catholic Statements and Background Works

Committee on the Laity, National Conference of Catholic Bishops. *Gifts Unfolding: The Lay Vocation Today with Questions for Tomorrow.* Washington, D.C.: United States Catholic Conference, 1990.

John Paul II. *The Vocation and Mission of the Lay Faithful (Christifedeles Laici).* Washington, D.C.: United States Catholic Conference, 1988.

Leckey, Dolores R. *Laity Stirring in the Church—Prophetic Questions.* Philadelphia: Fortress Press, 1987.

National Conference of Catholic Bishops. *Called and Gifted for the Third Millennium* (Reflections on the 30th Anniversary of the Decree on the Apostolate of the Laity and the 15th Anniversary of *Called and Gifted*). Washington, D.C.: United States Catholic Conference, 1996.

Osborne, Kenan, OFM. *Ministry: Lay Ministry in the Roman Catholic Church*. New York/Mahwah: Paulist Press, 1993.

Second Vatican Council. *Decree on the Apostolate of the Laity (Apostolicam Actuositatem)*. Washington, D.C.: United States Catholic Conference, 1965.

Skapanski, Gene A. *The Role of the Laity in the Context of* Communio *and Mission in Selected Vatican and World Council of Churches Documents 1967–1987*. Rome: Pontifical University St. Thomas, 1988.

Sofield, Loghlan and Donald Kuhn. *The Collaborative Leader: Listening to the Wisdom of God's People*. Notre Dame, Ind.: Ave Maria Press, 1995.

Ecumenical Documents Series

Volume I, *Doing the Truth in Charity* (New York/Mahwah: Paulist Press, 1982). Thomas Stransky and John B. Sheerin, eds. Includes Vatican and papal documents 1964-1980.

Volume II, *Growth in Agreement* (New York/Mahwah: Paulist Press, 1984). Harding Myer and Lukas Vischer, eds. Provides reports and statements of international ecumenical dialogues.

Volume III, *Towards the Healing of Schism: The Sees of Rome and Constantinople* (New York/Mahwah: Paulist Press, 1987). E. J. Stormion, SJ, ed. Statements and correspondence 1958-84.

Volume IV, *Building Unity* (New York/Mahwah: Paulist Press, 1988). Joseph Burgess and Jeffrey Gros, FSC, eds. Includes joint statements of dialogues with Roman Catholic participation, especially in USA, 1965–1986.

Volume V, *Growing Consensus: Church Dialogues in the U.S. 1962-1991* (New York/Mahwah: Paulist Press, 1995). Includes Protestant, Catholic, Orthodox, Evangelical, and Faith and Order statements.